You Can
Go Home Again

You Can
Go Home Again

◆

Johnny Majors
with Ben Byrd

Rutledge Hill Press
Nashville, Tennessee

Published in Nashville, Tennessee, by Rutledge Hill Press, Inc., 513 Third Avenue South, Nashville, Tennessee 37210

Typography by ProtoType Graphics, Inc., Nashville, Tennessee

Permission to reprint photographs is gratefully acknowledged of the following: Elizabeth Majors; Mary Lynn Barnwell Majors; Bob Dillon; *The Knoxville Journal;* The University of Tennessee Center for Educational Video and Photography; The University of Tennessee Athletic Department; Iowa State University Department of Intercollegiate Athletics; The University of Pittsburgh Department of Athletics; Mississippi State University Department of Athletics; and The University of Arkansas Department of Athletics.

Library of Congress Cataloging-in-Publication Data

Majors, Johnny, 1935–
  You can go home again.

  1. Majors, Johnny, 1935–   . 2. Football—
United States—Coaches—Biography.   I. Byrd, Ben.
II. Title.
GV939.M285A3   1986   796.332′092′4   [B]   86-17815
ISBN 0-934395-28-4

Manufactured in the United States of America
    1 2 3 4 5 6 7 8 9 10 — 91 90 89 88 87 86

To my family, those gone and those still living:

> They have given me life,
> have supported and sustained me,
> continue to bring joy to my days,
> and give me reason to look forward to tomorrow.

In memory of:

Shirley Inman Majors (May 7, 1913—April 5, 1981)
Bill Majors (November 7, 1938—October 18, 1965)

CONTENTS

You Can
Go Home Again

✦ 1 ✦

Home Again!

How quickly the time had passed.

Twenty-nine years.

And now, once again, I was headed home.

As I sat on the plane, I found myself thinking back over those years. They had been filled with so much.

A brief career in professional football in Canada. Assistant coaching at Tennessee. Meeting Mary Lynn and raising a family. More assistant coaching at Mississippi State and Arkansas. My first head coaching job at Iowa State, a national championship at Pittsburgh. And then Tennessee. Always Tennessee.

Life had been good to me.

Yet the years had not been without their difficulties. I thought of my brother Bill and my father, both now dead, and wished they could have been there to share in the glory. I remembered the days when I wondered if I'd ever be a head coach, and the days I wondered why I had wanted to be one. I recalled the hard work of building up three football programs. Especially the painfully slow struggle at Tennessee and the disappointment many friends and fans had felt.

But this was a time for celebrating, and the plane was filled with excitement. We had just beaten a fine University of Miami team in the Sugar Bowl. Picked to lose by most of the experts, we had dominated the game and had won by a lopsided 35–7 score. The victory still tasted sweet, and we were headed home.

Winners.

Winners for Tennessee!

+ + +

I couldn't help but remember an earlier Sugar Bowl game on New Year's Day, 1957. Then Bowden Wyatt was the coach and I a player. How I admired and respected that man! He had turned us into a disciplined, productive football team. It was he who had offered me my first coaching job. He had been my benefactor and my friend.

I also found myself thinking back over the years since I had returned to Tennessee, the good and bad times, the struggles and triumphs. What Thomas Wolfe said was true, up to a point. It *is* hard to go home again. But with a loving family, good friends, a lot of help, and some luck along the way, it can be done.

When the team plane landed at the Knoxville airport, the first person to greet us was Mrs. Bowden Wyatt. Molly was wearing Coach Wyatt's old orange and white Tennessee letter sweater, with three stripes and a captain's star on the left sleeve. She gave me a great big hug.

"Welcome home, Johnny," she said.

And I was.

✦2✦

The First Coach Majors

My mother says I could throw and bounce a ball before I walked.

I inherited my abilities. Daddy was a natural athlete, as good as any I ever coached, and my little mom, all four-feet-ten of her, to this day is a fierce competitor, with one of the coolest minds I've known.

Daddy was named Shirley Inman Majors, my mother John Elizabeth Bobo Majors. The *John* was a family tradition; her father and grandfather were both named John E. Bobo. That unusual combination many years later prompted my good friend Duffy Daugherty, football's greatest humorist, to introduce me at a banquet as "the only coach in the country with a father named Shirley and a mother named John." Actually, everybody has always called mother Elizabeth.

I was born in Lynchburg, Tennessee—the home of Jack Daniel's Whiskey—in the house of my mother's widowed mother, Bessie Bobo. Mother and Daddy had been living with his parents, Mr. and Mrs. John William Majors, about ten miles west of Lynchburg, but we soon moved to Lynchburg to live with Grandmother Bobo. It was there, in a frame house one block off the town square, that the Majors clan was reared. I was the oldest, born May 21, 1935. Brother Joe was born a year and a half later, and then Bill, two years after that. Shirley Ann, my only sister, was born a year and a half later. After a little over a year, Larry was born. Bob, the baby, was almost an afterthought, born when I was fourteen and already in high school.

Because only six years separated Larry and me, we looked like an assembly line when we went out in public. I was a very sensitive kid, and I used to get embarrassed when my brothers and sister tagged along behind me single file. Once when we went into Tullahoma, the nearest "big" town, I complained, "Mother, why won't you make us all stay together so we don't look so strung out?"

Daddy was the first Coach Majors. I have often wondered how he became such a good coach. He never played college football and was a farmer and barber for several years before he started coaching in high school. Even then, it was sort of an accident.

During World War II there was a shortage of coaches everywhere, and Lynchburg High School was unable to field a team in 1943. Therefore the high school players put on a drive selling scrap iron and scrap paper to raise enough money to pay Daddy to coach the team in 1944.

He had been a remarkable athlete in high school. Mother still has his old scrapbooks, and I remember a press clipping from a Lynchburg–Tullahoma game that said, "Majors ran like a ghost." I can believe it. One day when I was a high school sophomore, Daddy challenged the whole squad in a 100-yard dash during practice and beat all of us easily. It wasn't even close. From what I've heard about him from people who played with him or saw him play, I figure he probably was the best football player of all the Majors.

Daddy left Lynchburg High School before his senior year. Those were Depression days, and he felt he needed to work. But Mr. Homer Laws, who became a great friend of the Majors family, was hired as principal of Englewood High in East Tennessee and talked Daddy into moving there to finish school and to play for the football team. He had a great season at Englewood, playing tailback, but he was never sought after by any colleges. Great players like him from small schools would not be overlooked today.

Daddy did not push any of us into sports. He didn't have to. He was involved in them long before he took up coaching, and we all wanted to follow in his footsteps. He played on the town independent baseball and basketball teams, often serving as coach or manager, and he officiated many school games. He always took us with him, and we learned from watching. Sometimes he would take us to the baseball diamond or the old gym in Lynchburg that was never locked and teach us how to hold a runner on base, or execute a double play, or keep the pivot foot planted so we wouldn't get called for traveling. He never made a big deal over teaching us the fine points of a game. It was just his nature to teach sports, and that is why he later became such an outstanding coach. It is what he was born to be.

All five of his sons played college football. I was a single wing tailback at Tennessee. Joe was a quarterback at Florida State, where some of his passing records stood until recently. Bill was an outstanding defensive player and played tailback for the Vols. Larry, the fastest, played tailback at Sewanee where Daddy coached. And Bob was a great defensive back and two-time All-American for Tennessee. I am sure we all had some natural ability. We were quicker and faster than most boys and were well-coordinated, but the early training we received from our dad was what made the difference.

My father was a tremendously positive influence in my life, and I know all my brothers would say the same. He not only pointed us toward football, which has brought me such great happiness, but he also showed us how to live a full, useful life. He enjoyed everything—his family, his work, his friends, hunting with his beloved bird dogs. He was a man of the earth. He knew the trees and the birds. And he loved life and lived it with zest.

I am proud of some of the things I have accomplished in my life, but as far as I am concerned, my dad was the real Coach Majors.

✦3✦

The Old Hometown

Lynchburg was home until I was fifteen years old. It hasn't changed very much over the years. It's a pretty little town of a few hundred people situated in the southern part of Middle Tennessee, thirty miles north of the Alabama state line. The Jack Daniel Distillery was the hub of the town's economic life, and still is. Thousands of tourists visit it every year.

We lived just off the northeast corner of the town square in Grandmother Bobo's house; the Moore County Public Library is there today. All the stores surround the square, where the county courthouse stands.

Moore County is the smallest county in Tennessee, and my family roots go back to its founding. My mother's great grandfather, John Pinckney Bobo, was a member of the committee that formed Moore County out of pieces of Franklin, Lincoln, and Bedford counties in the nineteenth century. His son, John E. Bobo, was involved in building the courthouse and the county jail.

Most people know me as Johnny Majors. My close friends call me John, but back in Lynchburg I always was called by both my first and middle names: John Terrill. To this day they call me John Terrill, and whenever someone calls out "John Terrill" I know it is someone from my old hometown.

Grandmother Bobo (we called her "Bobo") lived in one side of the house, and the Majors clan in the other. She had an indomitable spirit, which she passed on to my mother. For years she and two other women operated the local telephone exchange, which she ran with an iron hand. Even the United States Army, much to its dismay, discovered that Bobo could not be pushed around. In the early days of World War II during one of the frequent war games held in the area, one of the armies invaded Lynchburg. An officer rapped on the door of the telephone office and informed her that his unit was taking over the exchange. "Not while I'm in charge, you're not," she replied. "Now, get out!" And he got out.

When I was just a little guy playing out in the yard, I had an excess of energy. I would play so hard that Bobo often exclaimed, "Elizabeth, John Terrill is going to die, his face is so red!" Well, I still go at things with the same sort of fury I did then, and my face still gets just as red.

I can thank my mother for that kind of energy and intensity. Even at her age she always has several things going at once. She paints, is a fine seamstress and a great cook, is an accomplished pianist, can do any kind of dance from the waltz to the twist, and is always involved in one kind of project or another. She never stops. I do not recall her ever taking a nap. It wasn't just that she had six kids and had to stay busy. She enjoyed life and her family, and she and Daddy gave us their time and love constantly. It was fun to be around both of them. They always were positive, and if they ever had any problems in life we kids certainly never heard about them.

As a young boy, I was very shy. I remember going to Halloween parties and staying outside because I was afraid my costume would not be as good as the other kids'. Finally, after listening to the good time the others were having, I would decide to join the fun. Once I was there, I always had as good a time as anyone.

Even though we only lived a block from downtown, Mother would get all dressed up in her best outfit on Saturday mornings and drive to the square. She was so short that she could barely see over the steering wheel. I was embarrassed about that and would lie down on the floorboard so nobody could see me. One day the man working at the service station looked up as we passed and almost fainted. "My goodness," he hollered, "there goes a car without a driver!"

When the time came to go to grade school, I got cold feet and refused to go. I had looked forward to it, but the reality scared me. I argued with Mother that there was no use in my going because I didn't know how to read, and she tried to explain that the reason for going was to learn to read. I wouldn't agree, and finally I broke down in tears and had to be dragged there. However, after that first day, I loved school and enjoyed every year of it, from first grade through college.

I also was shy about wearing short pants as a kid because I thought my legs looked too funny to be exposed to public view. It took both parents to get them on me, Daddy holding me while mother pulled them on.

Although I was bashful in some situations, I was rather assertive in others. I almost always was the one who organized the games for the boys my age, whether it was baseball, football, or something like hide-and-seek or kick-the-can.

As the oldest child, I probably was guilty of bossing my brothers and sister too much. Since World War II was in progress at the time, playing war was one of our favorite pastimes, especially for brothers Joe and Bill and me. As the self-appointed king of the hill, I always played the part of the United States forces. Finally one day Bill, who had a stubborn streak in him, rebelled. "I'm tired of being Germany and Japan," he said. "I'm not going to play this game any more unless I can be America!"

With Camp Forrest so near, at Tullahoma, the war seemed quite close to us. We always got excited when the maneuvers brought the troops into Lynchburg. Sometimes they even brought their tanks into town and set up machine gun nests in the town square.

During the summers when we spent a lot of time at Grandmother Majors' farm at Beech Hill, the soldiers often carried out their war games on her farm and nearby. The soldiers always seemed to be hot and thirsty, so Joe and I often ran up to the spring house to bring them a jug of cold water. They usually gave us a tip of a dime or a quarter. Selling drinking water to our nation's soldiers seems awful now, but as far as we were concerned it was pure old American free enterprise at work.

The war brought restrictions on what the people at home could get. Gasoline, tires, sugar, and a lot of other things were rationed. To a ten-year-old boy, the bubble gum shortage was one of the cruelest. For years there was no bubble gum to be found in Moore County. Then one day in 1945 I got word that the restrictions had been eased and there would be some bubble gum available before long. I called every grocery store in town for weeks. Finally, one day I called Tolley's Service Station and was told that some bubble gum was expected that afternoon. I don't know when I had been so excited.

This was too big a secret to keep to myself, so I told three of my best buddies: my brother Joe; Kenny Harrison, whose father owned the funeral home on the southwest corner of the square; and David "Chicken" Cunningham, who lived down the street. I warned them not to tell anybody else. When school was out that day, we jumped on our bikes and headed for Tolley's, which was about a mile out of town. When we got within a few hundred yards of Tolley's, Chicken Cunningham started peddling like a mad man. Before we could react and catch up with him, he was already at the store.

When we arrived, we went in and asked for the bubble gum. "I had about twenty pieces, but this young man bought up them all," he said, pointing to Chicken.

"Chicken," I demanded, "we've got to divide up that bubble gum."

"No way," he said. "I bought it, and it's mine."

"You didn't even know about it until I told you," I hollered, "so now you've got to split it with the rest of us."

Chicken said, "I got here first, and it's mine."

I had waited too long for that bubble gum to lose it, so Chicken and I went to the mat, and he ended up agreeing to a four-way split. All four of us have laughed about that incident many times since then.

We Majors had a lot of friends in that little town, and we played together everywhere, in our yard, on the school ball field, and sometimes in Cousin Mattie Bobo's big side yard across the street. Brothers Joe and Bill, nearest to me in age, were my closest friends; Shirley Ann and Larry, who were just a year apart, played together most of the time. They got along just great almost always, but when they fought it was pure war. They were both hotheaded and stubborn, and when they fought you could hear the battle all over Lynchburg.

Today I appreciate my brothers and sister more than ever. If anything, we are closer now than we were as children. They are my best and truest friends, and I am very thankful that we have stayed in close touch as adults.

❖4❖
Play Ball

I have loved sports for as long as I can remember.

I saw my first basketball game in the old, barnlike gym at Lynchburg High School. I was two years old, and my father was one of the referees. At half time I managed to get hold of the game ball and ran out on the floor bouncing it and trying to shoot it at the basket the way the real players had been doing. When they took the ball away from me so the second half could begin, I made a terrible struggle. Mother says that just tickled Daddy to death.

Shirley Majors, with his boys tagging along behind him at a ballgame, became a familiar scene in Lynchburg and nearby towns. Frank Bobo, a distant cousin, says he can't remember ever seeing Daddy at a sporting event without us.

By the time Daddy began coaching at Lynchburg High, I was nine years old and always underfoot at practice and at the games. Daddy was a lot more patient and understanding than some coaching fathers would have been. Joe, Bill, and I usually organized pickup games at half time of high school games and we had to go to the dressing room to ask Daddy for a ball. That's a terrible time to bother a football coach; but Daddy would snap at us a little and then give us one. "Take it and get out of here," he'd say.

Daddy was an incurable sports fan himself. Several times each summer he would load us into the car and drive us to Nashville, usually with two or three friends of his, to see the Nashville Vols play baseball at the old Sulphur Dell park. Sometimes we were able to see the Vols play an exhibition game against a major league club. That was the biggest thrill of all. We got to see the Detroit Tigers when Hank Greenberg was their star slugger and the Boston Red Sox when the great Ted Williams played left field for them. I still can call off the Red Sox starting lineup when they visited Nashville in 1946, the year they won the American League pennant.

When we went to a ball game with Daddy, we went to see the ball game. It wasn't like going on a picnic. We got a couple of soft drinks and a hot dog, and that was it. We always arrived early, too. If it was a baseball game, he wanted to watch batting practice and infield practice. If it was a football game, he wanted to be there when the teams took the field for pre-game practice. He enjoyed the game, but he was always the coach, always the critic. He analyzed the games and explained what was happening as they took place.

The first football game I ever saw was the Vanderbilt–Ole Miss game at Dudley Stadium in Nashville when I was twelve years old. Jimmy Eanes, a sporting goods salesman and a good friend of Daddy's, got us tickets. He also gave me my first pair of football cleats when I was a freshman at Lynchburg High School.

I'll always remember that game. Not only was it my first game, but it contained an unusual play that helped determine the outcome. Ole Miss featured the great passing combination of Charlie Conerly to Barney Poole, and on the play in question Poole caught a pass for an apparent touchdown. However, it had been tipped by one of his teammates and was ruled incomplete. Vandy won the game, 10–6, but if today's rules had been in effect the touchdown would have counted and Ole Miss would have been the winner.

I followed Vanderbilt football much more closely than Tennessee in those years. Nashville was much closer to home than Knoxville, and I never dreamed that some day I would play for the Vols. As a matter of fact, Alabama also ranked ahead of Tennessee with me. I followed those great wartime Alabama teams, with stars like Harry Gilmer, Vaughn Mancha, and Lowell Tew, in the newspapers and on radio broadcasts.

My favorite team in those years was Army, which had the great Doc Blanchard and Glenn Davis, "Mr. Inside and Mr. Outside," under Coach Earl "Red" Blaik. Every Saturday in the fall I would hurry to complete my morning chores; I got fifty cents a week for carrying coal and coal oil to Miss Ann Dance's house. Then I would run downtown to buy a soda pop and a couple of candy bars, and then curl up by the radio to listen to the play-by-play broadcast of the Army game. The Cadets dominated their games so strongly then that hardly anyone ever played them to a close game. They were my idols.

I was also a big basketball fan in those years, and still am. My favorite team in the late '40s was Kentucky's Fabulous Five, with Alex Groza, Ralph Beard, and Wah Wah Jones. I listened to their games on the radio on winter nights. One of my greatest thrills was to travel to Nashville with Daddy to see that great Kentucky team play Vanderbilt in the old East High gym. Even while I was playing football at Tennessee, I always got to the Alumni Memorial gym early so I could get a good seat when the Kentucky basketball team came to town with Cliff Hagan and Frank Ramsey. My daddy had taught me I should always respect greatness, even when it's on your opponent's side.

Seeing and hearing about the great teams and great players fired my imagination and, like so many other boys, I played out my fantasies on the sandlots. Cousin Mattie Bobo's yard became Yankee Stadium in the summer and the Rose Bowl in the fall. The first time I ever hit a line drive that cleared the street running past our makeshift diamond, I went into a home run trot that would have made Ted Williams proud. But you can't live forever on dreams alone, and I was itching to play in real games on real teams.

I hurried the schedule along by organizing the Lynchburg grade school basketball team when I was in sixth grade. I talked the county agent, Mr. Tolley, into getting us tee shirts with *Lynchburg* printed on the front. We were extremely proud of that. He also arranged a schedule with other schools in the county, like Hurdlow, Lois, and Harmony. Our first game was played against a grade school team from Hurdlow, on an outdoor court. In those days the Future Farmers of America sponsored basketball teams, and I joined up so I could play with them, even though I was a town boy. By the time I was eleven, I was involved in several types of sports competition.

I still was very sensitive, and misfortune on the playing field absolutely crushed me. One day when I was in the sixth or seventh grade, I made a mistake in a softball game at Fayetteville. I was pitching, and we were leading by one run in the last inning. Fayetteville had a runner on third; and wanting to be sure of the situation, I asked how many outs there were. Their coach, who was coaching at third base, said there were two outs. The batter hit the ball back to me, and I threw to first base for what I thought was the game-ending out. It turned out that it was only the second out, and we ended up losing. I felt I had been misled and cried like a baby. I was so embarrassed I wanted to go off somewhere and hide, and I was furious at the Fayetteville coach. But to tell the truth, I don't know whether he deliberately fooled me or if it was an honest mistake.

Another incident was even more embarrassing. It happened the first time I ever played against one of my father's teams. I was in the ninth grade at Lynchburg and was playing on the high school varsity basketball team, which gives you some idea of how good we were not. By this time Daddy was coaching Huntland High—basketball and football—and I was excited about going to Huntland to play against his team.

The game was very close in the first half, and when we came out for the second half I was all fired up to do real well. I got the ball on the tipoff and drove downfloor, making a beautiful layup—for Huntland. I had forgotten that we were defending a different goal in the second half. I went over to the bench, sat down, and cried my heart out. My coach had to call time-out for a couple of minutes so I could compose myself to get back out on the floor.

My first organized football occurred when I was in the seventh and eighth grades at Lynchburg. Skippy Parks, a longtime friend of the Majors family, donated his services as coach. We weren't a very good team and I didn't learn much about the fine points of the game, but I did learn one valuable lesson. Football is a contact sport, and anyone who thinks he wants to play it has to come to terms with that reality.

Some high school freshmen who were not good enough to make the varsity were allowed to play with the seventh and eighth graders. One day a ninth grader, about twice as big as I, hit me very hard. I'm not sure whether I was addled or whether

I just didn't want to take another hit like that, but I asked Skippy to take me out of the game.

I played another eight years of football without experiencing a whole lot of fear about the physical aspect of the game, but I don't want to give a false, macho impression. I never enjoyed taking hard licks, and I didn't play football to prove to myself or anybody else how tough I was. In fact, it always was the other way around. Part of the challenge to me as a running back was to avoid the contact. It is the nature of the tackler to establish contact and the nature of the ball carrier to elude it.

I always was very happy with the role I played.

⋆5⋆

At Home

The Majors family never lived a one-dimensional life. Our interests were many and varied.

Mother had a hand in just about every kind of undertaking. Daddy probably loved sports as much as anybody who ever lived, but he enjoyed many other things as well. He enjoyed being a barber, and took pride in being a good one. The fact that he gave it up to become a football coach indicates how fierce his drive to coach was. When he entered coaching during World War II, he was prospering as a barber as he never had previously. He was co-owner of his own shop in Tullahoma, and the many soldiers stationed at Camp Forrest kept him busy all the time. When it came time to coach the boys at Lynchburg High School, he sold his interest in the shop so they could have a coach.

Daddy and Mother both were "people" people. They loved living in a small town, with all the give-and-take of the informal social life. Daddy was a great practical joker, with a number of friends who enjoyed that sort of thing. Whenever anyone pulled a good one, he usually was involved.

Once Bill "Dude" Daniels and two or three other guys "auctioned off" Daddy's cow. Bill was an auctioneer, and close to midnight one night he and his friends drove up to our house. Bill got out his auctioneer's loudspeaker and began taking "bids" on the cow. One guy would holler out a figure, and Bill would start chanting it. Windows all over town went up so folks could see what was happening. Finally, Daddy got out his shot-gun and fired a couple of blasts into the trees over everybody's head. The auction came to a sudden end.

Occasionally Daddy borrowed a mule from our next door neighbor, Mr. Grammar, to plow a garden patch at our house. One day when Daddy went to lunch after plowing a good part of the morning, Alf Cashion, who worked at Price's Service Station, took advantage of the opportunity. He led the mule to a barn somewhere outside of town, where he hid it. When Daddy returned home, the mule was gone. Now it was an unwritten rule that you never acknowledged being the victim of a practical joke, so Daddy never breathed a word about it. It was several days before anyone told him where the mule was.

That led to a second incident. Alf usually walked when he had to go downtown, but one day he drove and parked his car on the town square. After finishing his business, he forgot that he had driven the car and walked back to the service station. When he got ready to leave work that evening, his car wasn't there. He was certain that Daddy had taken it, but he wouldn't say a word. He just walked wherever he had to go. After several days one of his friends asked, "Alf, did you know that your car has been parked down at the square for a week?"

I inherited or acquired my parents' enthusiasm for life. I, too, am interested in many different things. I love reading, especially history and biography. I love traveling, especially with my family. I love music—popular, country and western, light classical, everything except hard rock. And, of course, I love people, sports, competition, talking, listening, and everything else that makes life so rich and full.

As a boy I took piano lessons from Mrs. Mary B. Parks, Skippy's mother. I enjoyed it, although football later crowded out the lessons. One of the most frightening things that happened to me in my childhood was my first piano recital. All of Mrs. Parks's students performed that day, and their parents were there at the school auditorium. I had practiced my piece until I felt like I knew it better than whoever wrote it. Standing in the wings waiting for my name to be called, I suddenly discovered that I couldn't recall one single note!

I was petrified. I knew I had only two choices. Either I could go out there on that stage and make a fool of myself, or I could sneak out the back door of the auditorium and never be seen again in Moore County. Then they called my name.

I squared my shoulders and walked onstage, ready for the slaughter. However, the instant I sat down at the piano, I discovered that I remembered every single note and zipped right through the music.

Not too many years later the same kind of stage fright struck me as I was getting ready to play my first high school football game. To tell the truth, to this day I have not completely gotten over that feeling. Every game brings that same old anxiety, and I am glad it does. It means that the game still matters to me.

·6·

High School Days

I was a scared fourteen-year-old as the Lynchburg High School football team took the field for the opening game of the 1949 season against Manchester. The same kind of panic that had almost set me running away from the piano recital grabbed me again, only much worse. Although I had been able to throw and kick spirals since I was five years old, in pregame practice that night they just wobbled end-over-end and died. I saw myself becoming the laughingstock of the town.

Fortunately Daddy, who was coaching Huntland High, had an open date that night and was watching me warm up. Standing in the end zone watching me, he knew what I was going through, so he called me over and asked what was bothering me.

"Daddy, I can't make the ball spiral passing or kicking," I answered.

He took that news very calmly. "I've got the idea that things will work out when the game starts," he said. "It's your first game, and it's only natural for you to be nervous about it."

He was right. As in the piano recital, it all came back to me once the game began. My punts spiraled, and I threw some spirals too; but most of them went to Manchester players. They made several interceptions and long runs and beat the wadding out of us, 58–0. This was just a preview of what was to come.

My coach at Lynchburg, Jack Brock, was a great guy who was awfully kind to me. He was from Kentucky originally and his specialty was basketball, so I got most of my football tutoring at night from my dad, who commuted about twenty miles daily to coach at Huntland. In midseason I was shifted to end on defense. I had no earthly idea how to play defensive end, but Daddy gave me a crash course in the living room. He showed me the proper stance and how to shuffle my feet and ward off blockers. Even though I learned a lot, it didn't help much when it came to fighting off boys who were thirty or forty pounds heavier than I.

Oddly enough, I scored my first touchdown as a defensive end. In our game against Chapel Hill, they threw a pass out in the flat on my side and I intercepted it. I ran it back down the sideline for about forty yards. My mother missed it. She attended the game, but at that moment she was out in the car changing my three-month-old brother Bob's diapers.

As we struggled through the fall, I learned how tough it is to go through a losing football season. We suffered some terrible defeats, losing to Tullahoma, 75–6, to Centerville, 33–0, to Chapel Hill, 39–7, and Pulaski, 65–7. We tried to maintain a positive attitude, but then the next game would come along and beat us down again. However, by hanging in there and not quitting, we learned how to do better in the future. I also learned that one doesn't have to have a winning season for football to be worthwhile. In many ways it parallels the rest of life, in which we must learn to deal with both adversity and triumph.

We did have one victory that fall. In the final game of the season we beat my dad's Huntland team, 19–13, and I scored two touchdowns. After the game Daddy said he wasn't ever going to get beat by one of his own boys again, so he moved his family to Huntland. By the time the 1950 season rolled around, I was a Huntland High Hornet.

Before the season started, the family rode back and forth from Lynchburg to practice with Daddy. As time for the first game neared, Mother pressed him to find us a place to live in Huntland. I had to be living in Huntland before I could go to school there, and I had to be enrolled in Huntland school before I could play football for it. We finally got a small apartment for a few weeks, and then we moved into a frame house just a block from downtown, pretty much like our home in Lynchburg. The two towns were, and still are, very much alike, small places filled with a few hundred of the finest people in the world.

The dynasty that Daddy established at Huntland hadn't started yet. Huntland had not had a football team for more than two decades when he took the job as coach in 1949, and he had to build the program from nothing. He lined off the gridiron and talked the students into sprigging grass for the field. Community participation played a big part in the success of the team, but we were a long way from being a successful team when I first took to the practice field there in August of 1950.

Huntland High School's great record of seventy wins and just one loss from 1950 through 1956 was a monument to my dad's coaching. We had good boys who gave a total effort, but it was his coaching genius that provided the extra. He was very much like Bowden Wyatt, my outstanding coach at Tennessee. Both taught the fundamentals well, both were direct, and both tolerated no nonsense. Neither had to scream and holler to let you know that you had done something wrong; all they had to do was look at you. All of us on the Huntland team dreaded the Majors "look" more than running laps or one-on-one drills. That included my brothers and me; we were treated just like everybody else, no better, no worse.

Daddy had played the old short punt formation under his Lynchburg High School coach, B. H. Thompson, the man he credited with teaching him the basics of the game. He was still using the short punt at Huntland in 1950, but he gradually worked single wing plays into the offense and wound up as a single wing coach. Both offenses are very similar in that they basically are built around the deep back, or tailback.

The four oldest Majors all played tailback on Daddy's teams. I played for three seasons, 1950 through 1952. Then Joe, who had been playing wingback, moved to tailback for the next two years. When Joe graduated, Bill moved over from fullback and was the tailback in 1955 and 1956. Larry was the tailback on his early teams at Sewanee. Brother Bob was the only one of us who never played for Daddy. By the time he reached high school, Daddy was coaching at Sewanee, and Bob played his college football at Tennessee.

Looking back, I am amazed at what our Huntland team was able to do in those years. As a coach I am deeply aware of how difficult it is to maintain that kind of consistency, game after game, year after year.

I was especially fortunate, for I was in the right place at the right time. I led the state of Tennessee in scoring all three seasons that I played, with 161 points as a sophomore, 153 as a junior, and 213 as a senior. In my senior year I scored thirty-five touchdowns, including quite a few long runs. The system helped me there. The way our team blocked on the off-tackle play often made it possible for me to break into the clear, and I was pretty good at open field running.

I don't know of any thrill in football that compares with the cutback run. As a runner, you sense when the defensive flow has overrun you and you cut back against the pursuers' flow and run to the open space. Daddy was a good teacher at how to run with the ball, and early in my career I learned to follow the guards on the wide plays. To a little skinny tailback like me, a good hard-blocking guard is the best friend he can have.

Daddy also taught me the old "limp leg" style of running, in which you show the tackler a leg and then pull it back and cut the other way. I guess running backs have been using that move to confuse would-be tacklers for as long as the game has been played.

The Huntland record drew a lot attention to the team and to me, and I picked up a new nickname in the process. Russ Melvin of the Nashville *Tennessean* covered our games, and when I scored three touchdowns in one game he wrote a story that led off, "John 'Drum' Majors leads Huntland victory." I became "Drum" to a lot of people after that, and when I started hearing from college recruiters, some of them addressed their letters to Drum Majors. Even in my early years at Tennessee I was called Drum, but gradually the name faded away and now I hardly ever hear it. I figure I have enough first names anyway with John, Johnny, and John Terrill.

Once we started winning big in 1950, the town of Huntland developed a special feeling toward the high school football team. Game day became a big celebration. Daddy had the shopkeepers playing fight music in the downtown stores, and townspeople would load us into cars and drive in a caravan to road games. Though I've had many thrills in football—winning the national championship at Pittsburgh, playing on Tennessee's great 1956 team, winning the Southeastern Conference title and the Sugar Bowl with the 1985 Tennessee team—I have never had a bigger thrill than beating Chapel Hill for the Duck River Valley Conference championship on a cold November night in 1950.

I remember the game vividly. It was played at Chapel Hill before an overflow crowd. On our first play from scrimmage our fullback, W. R. "Slats" McCreeless, moved into the blocking back slot and got the ball on a trick play. Slats took it about fifty yards to the one-yard line. We scored from there and stayed ahead the entire game, winning 34–14, to complete a 10-0 season. We were invited to the first postseason game Huntland ever played in, the Little Bowl at Winchester, in which we beat Jo Byrns High, 20–13. I was fortunate to be able to return a punt for the winning touchdown.

It was amazing the way Daddy was able to take a team that was only in its second year of football to an 11–0 record, and the excitement it created in Huntland was just as amazing. The next season, 1951, we were undefeated again and drew even more attention from the press. The father/son angle was played up big, and the *Nashville Banner* had a special section on us, with a full-page picture of the team lined up in the single wing formation. An artist had drawn Hornets dropping bombs to get the team nickname in. We all knew it was coming out, and it seemed as though almost everyone in Huntland was at the post office waiting for the mail delivery that brought the *Banner* to town.

Our winning streak continued into my senior season of 1952. We escaped one upset because my dad knew when to bear down. Petersburg led us at half time on our own field, and I was hobbling around with a slight groin injury. At half time Daddy told every player individually that he wasn't playing the kind of game that he should and let him know what he expected from him in the second half. When he got to me, he said, "And you, young man, you had better get that limp out of that leg in the second half." He knew that I was hurt a little, but not really injured. Actually, he used a little more salty language than that, and I had no trouble getting the point.

The Huntland field was not perfectly level, and we went into the last three minutes of the game still trailing and facing eighty yards of uphill terrain. Nevertheless we put the winning drive together to pull it out by a couple of points. I think every one of us could still hear Daddy's half time remarks ringing in our ears. Ever since then, I've always believed the fourth quarter belongs to me and have coached my teams to believe that it belongs to them. Whenever we have needed to pull out a victory—like in the Alabama game in 1984—my mind goes back to that Petersburg game in 1952.

We finally lost a game that season, to my old school, Lynchburg, 13–0. It was the only defeat in my three seasons at Huntland. My brother Bill played for four years under Daddy, and he never played in a losing game.

This past July the Huntland High School football field was named after my dad, and the Majors family was on hand for the dedication. It was the kind of memorial he would have liked. His heart was always there, with his players. I could not help but remember how many times he had put his boys through football practice on that field, then loaded into his car the boys who didn't have a ride and drove them home, sometimes way out in the country. Shirley Majors was more than a coach to his players. He was a friend.

·7·

An Assist from Mother

Football was not the only thing in life for me at Huntland High, or anywhere else. I enjoyed school and was a good student with above average grades. A member of the Beta Club, I also was active in the Drama Club and had parts in several school plays, which I enjoyed very much. In addition, I learned how to handle that basic subject, English, from one of the great teachers of all time, Miss Nell Baker.

Miss Nell taught both English and history, and she kept us up with current events. She had us memorize great literature, from Chaucer to Shakespeare, and she also assigned us to read the *New York Times* in the school library. She wanted us to know about the world that lay outside our little corner of Tennessee. At our thirtieth class reunion at Huntland High in 1983, I led off my talk with the Prologue from *The Canterbury Tales*. All of us could relate to that because all of Miss Nell's students had to memorize it.

I have always been fascinated by distant places that lie beyond the horizon. When I was a junior at Huntland High, I began organizing a trip to Washington, D. C., for the following year. We sold magazines, and furniture polish to raise the money to pay for the trip, and I won a prize for selling the most. We were unable to afford a chartered bus, so we made the trip in an old yellow school bus. My mother went along to help our class sponsor, Mrs. Margie Kennedy, and "Brother" James Harney, one of our teachers, went as the boys' escort. We had a great time. We visited all the historical sites, and some of us boys went to a Washington Senators baseball game. They played the Cleveland Indians, and I was absolutely delighted that one of the greatest pitchers of all time, Bob Feller, pitched for the Indians that day. For a sports fan like me, that alone would have made the trip worthwhile.

My first date was with Dorothy Jared when I was a freshman at Lynchburg. I was as nervous as could be, and I didn't know whether to try to hold her hand or kiss her or what when I told her goodnight. So I didn't do anything. The girl I dated most frequently was Dorothy Holt, who grew up close by in Lynchburg. Dorothy had sisters the same ages as my brothers Joe and Bill, and it became the natural thing for the Majors boys and the Holt girls to go out together. Dorothy later went to the University of Tennessee at the same time I did, and we dated some there, too. She is now Mrs. Rudy Elam, and she and her husband are among the good friends I always visit when I am in Lynchburg.

Mr. Homer Laws was our principal at Huntland High. He was the man who talked Daddy into finishing high school at Englewood, and it was he who persuaded him to take the coaching job. Mr. Laws was an outstanding principal, and he ran a happy school.

I once disappointed Mr. Laws during a basketball game, and it was terribly embarrassing to me. We were playing Petersburg, a strong rival, and I thought the officials were treating us wrong. There's something about basketball that makes me get much madder at the officials than in football. The officials called me for traveling when I didn't think I had, and a short time later I was called for it again. This time I threw the ball down as hard as I could, and it bounced off the ceiling. The referee should have called a technical on me, but he didn't. Later in the game he also called my brother Joe for traveling, and Joe slammed the ball against the floor. Following his big brother's example, I guess.

The next day Mr. Laws called me into his office and said, "It embarrassed me to see you do that, John. You don't want to do anything like that anymore." I felt about two feet tall, and that was the last time I ever threw a tantrum as a player.

As I approached the end of high school, the matter of deciding where to go to college grew more important. I had a great year in football, rushing for 2,550 yards and averaging 17.7 yards per carry; so I was getting a lot of attention from college recruiters. I certainly was not an imposing physical specimen at five feet, eleven inches, and just over 150 pounds, but my statistics were impressive and I had received some publicity by being named Midstate Player of the Year and making the All-State team.

Most of the Southeastern Conference schools contacted me, as well as others from some far-flung locations like Wyoming, West Point, Arkansas, and Virginia Tech. However, neither Alabama or Georgia Tech contacted me, although I would have been interested in them, especially Alabama which I had always followed so closely.

I still have some of the letters I received from college coaches. One that was naturally very important to me was from Coach Paul Bryant of Kentucky, who was fast becoming a legend, even then. The correspondence from Wyoming was signed by Assistant Coach John "Skeeter" Bailey. That was the start of what has been a long and close friendship.

Skeeter Bailey was on Bowden Wyatt's Wyoming staff at the time, later moving on to Arkansas and then to Tennessee with Coach Wyatt. Skeeter had heard about me through C. T. Hewgley, who went to Wyoming earlier from our part of the country. I was flattered by the attention from Wyoming, but it seemed an awfully long way from home, so I decided to stay in the South.

Three years later, when I had completed my first two seasons at Tennessee, Bowden Wyatt was chosen to succeed Harvey Robinson as the head coach at Tennessee. He brought Skeeter and most of his other assistants with him. When I met the coaching staff for the first time at the football banquet in January of 1955, Skeeter's eyes lit up when I was introduced. "Damn your little skinny soul," he laughed. "I finally caught up with your ass!"

I made my first recruiting visit to Mississippi State while I was a junior. In those days college teams could put you in uniform and pads and run you through some drills on the field. I threw the ball, ran some pass patterns, and kicked a few balls. It amounted to a tryout, and I guess I did all right because they recruited me pretty heavily after that. Murray Warmath, an old

Tennessee player who later had some great teams at Minnesota, was the head coach.

Coach Warmath was the sharpest dresser I had ever seen. He wore a nifty outfit, a suit, a straw hat, and two-tone shoes that had taps on them. I thought those taps were really uptown. A long time later, after I came back to Tennessee as head coach, I invited him down to meet with our staff and critique our program. During the conversation I said, "Coach Warmath, I'll never forget those taps you had on your shoes the first time I met you." He leaned back in his chair, put his feet on the table, and there they were.

My recruiting visits enabled me to see a little bit of the world. Georgia had me come down to Athens for a visit, and I got to see the Georgia-Georgia Tech game between the hedges in 1952. Tech had a great team that year, and they won. I corresponded quite a bit with Hobe Hooser of the Florida staff. Florida's head coach then was Bob Woodruff, who later became my athletic director at Tennessee.

My father's mother, who was Ella Sanders before she married, was a cousin of Red Sanders, who had done such a fine job as head coach at Vanderbilt before moving on to UCLA. While I never met him, my father knew him. Fred Russell of the *Nashville Banner* has frequently commented to me that he has long wondered whether I would have gone to Vanderbilt if Coach Sanders had still been there when I graduated from high school.

As time went on, I narrowed my choice to fewer and fewer schools, until finally there were just two left, Auburn and Tennessee. I thought about Auburn for a long while because I liked my visit there. Auburn had a small town flavor like Lynchburg or Huntland, and I thought I would be comfortable there. However, it didn't turn out that way.

Mother was more responsible for my choosing Tennessee than any other person. Neither of my parents ever tried to tell me where I should go, but when I finally told them I was having a hard time deciding between Tennessee and Auburn, Mother said, "Well, if there's not any big difference one way or the other, I'd just as soon you stayed in the state."

And that was all it took.

•8•

Tennessee Bound

Farmer Johnson showed up at Spring practice between my junior and senior seasons of high school. Although I had never met him, of course I knew who he was, the defensive coordinator for General Neyland and one of the most highly respected assistant coaches in college football.

He asked my dad to let me do a few things for him. He had me run off tackle on Huntland's version of Tennessee's famous "10" play, and I also ran the pass-run option and did some punting and fielding of kicks. When we finished, he asked me if I would like to come to Knoxville for Tennessee's game with Alabama in the fall. That was the first I knew Tennessee was interested in me.

As a kid I had never entertained any thoughts of playing for Tennessee. Because the tradition was so great and the school seemed so big, I was in awe of it. In fact, I did not see the Vols play until 1950, when they beat Alabama, 14–9. John Hunter, who ran a general hardware store in Huntland, Daddy, and I rode to Knoxville with Ray Johnson, who owned the sawmill, in Ray's big black Lincoln. I sat in a student seat, Section C. The Vols won the game with the old "hip" play as wingback Ed Morgan took the ball from tailback Herky Payne and made a long run down the east sidelines to the south goal.

Daddy and I were so impressed with the game that we went to Birmingham the next season to see the 1951 game at Legion Field. The Vols were national champions that year and, of course, they won again. Hank Lauricella hit Bert Rechichar in the end zone with a touchdown pass.

By that time I had seen several college games, but nothing equaled Tennessee versus Alabama. Since then I have taken part in many more, but I still get that old breathless feeling when the Volunteers tee it up against the Crimson Tide. I appreciate all the things that television has done for college football, but there is one pre-TV feature of this series which I wish we could bring back. I'd like to see Tennessee in orange jerseys and Alabama in red the way it was when I first saw them play. There was something about seeing school color against school color that was lost when visiting teams were made to wear white.

When I accepted Farmer Johnson's invitation to the 1952 game, it was the third time I had seen Tennessee play, each time against Alabama. The Vols won this game too, 20–0; and Jimmy Wade, who was to be one of my teammates two years later, scored all three touchdowns. That team was General Neyland's last at Tennessee. He became ill late in the season, and Harvey Robinson coached the team in the Cotton Bowl against Texas. He was named head coach the following year.

Because of his illness, I never got to play for General Neyland, but he still was the coach when I signed and I've always felt that I was one of his "boys." To tell the truth, I don't think he was all that impressed with me when he got his first look at me, and I didn't blame him. I sure didn't *look* like I could run over any big defensive tackles.

My dad and I went back to Knoxville to see Tennessee play Kentucky late in the 1952 season. It was snowing that day, and we arrived too late to see Ray Byrd's long touchdown run in the first quarter of a 14–14 tie. We stayed over that night and then visited the athletic dorm in East Stadium on Sunday morning. That was the first time I met the general. Farmer Johnson introduced us to him in a little offset room where he always had breakfast. I was so awed by him that I can't remember much of what he said; but just meeting him helped move me a lot closer to signing with Tennessee.

The state championship Isaac Litton High School team of Nashville was also visiting Knoxville that weekend, and that was the first time I met John Gordy who was a star tackle on that team. John was regarded as the top lineman in Tennessee that year. Four years later John was the captain and I was the alternate captain of an undefeated Tennessee team.

Even after I signed with Tennessee, I had a hard time convincing myself that I would be good enough to play for the Vols. I was very conscious of my size, or lack of it; and I spent much of the summer before I entered school trying to build myself up physically. John Hunter got me a job on a road gang, digging ditches and laying tile. But as the time to head to Knoxville drew near, my anxiety got worse. I had nightmare after nightmare about failing. I was afraid I would be embarrassed. I could see myself being the worst player on the freshman team.

It got so bad that Daddy finally sat me down one day and gave me some straight talk. "See here, young man," he said. "You're worried about playing for Tennessee. The way you can run the football, you can play for anybody."

I still had lots of doubts, but Daddy's talk sure helped me. Later I felt the same sort of anxiety about my first head coaching job at Iowa State. Now I realize that the sun is going to come up tomorrow no matter what happens on the football field. But I still have pregame jitters, as I think most coaches and players have.

The day I left Huntland for Knoxville was a tough day for the Majors family. I was the first of the children to leave home, and Knoxville seemed a million miles away. I had tears in my eyes, and I could see the ones Mother had in hers. She later told me that even though Daddy tried not to show any emotion at the time, later he went out in the backyard and cried when nobody was looking.

Daddy drove me to Shelbyville and fitted me out in a new suit. I rode to Knoxville from there with Miss Cora Stovall, who was going back to Kingsport to teach after spending the summer at home with her sister, who ran a grocery store in town.

When we got to Knoxville, she let me out in front of East Stadium dorm. I don't think I've ever felt as lonely as I did at that moment. There I was, the small town boy in the big city.

I kept thinking, "What am I doing here?" And I didn't have any answers.

✦9✦

The Littlest Freshman

I was picked to be the quarterback on the freshman "scout" team. We ran the plays our opponents were expected to run, and since all our opponents ran the T formation, I became a T quarterback for the season. Our backfield unit consisted of Bob Hibbard and Bob Smithers at the halfback spots and Lon Herzbrun as fullback.

I have never known how many freshmen Tennessee recruited for the 1953 season, although some people have said 127. At that time there were no limits on scholarships, and the Vols were trying to replace most of the players from the great teams of the previous three seasons. The practice field was thick with freshmen, and I was the smallest of the bunch. I was even smaller after two weeks of practice, weighing 144 pounds.

Our first freshman–varsity scrimmage was a big event in my life. I still had a lot of doubts about whether or not I could make it, and the thought of going up against defensive linemen like Darris McCord and Roger Rotroff did little to calm my fears. McCord was big and tough, and Rotroff was tough and vicious. I soon learned to be aware of where he lined up, just as later in my career I always knew where guys like Larry Morris of Georgia Tech and Lou Michaels of Kentucky were.

It was during that scrimmage that I first realized I could play football at Tennessee. After I got the feel of it, I began to find some chinks in the varsity defense. First I made a pretty nice seven-yard gain. Then I got loose for a fifteen-yard run. As I picked myself up from the ground, I thought, "I'm making these guys miss me!"

At one break in the action I heard a commanding voice asking, "Who's that number ten?" It was General Neyland, who was sitting in the lower part of the west side of Neyland Stadium.

Farmer Johnson yelled out, as loud as he could, "General, that's Majors. From Huntland!"

Farmer had taken a lot of kidding from some of the other coaches, and probably from Neyland himself, for signing me. I guess he was thrilled because he felt vindicated. As for me, I was thrilled because I wasn't dead.

As soon as the practice was finished, I hurried straight to Ellis and Ernest drugstore to call home, collect. "Daddy," I reported, "they miss tackles up here just like they do in high school!"

As all freshmen before and since have discovered, I soon found out that I was just so much raw meat for the varsity to chew on in scrimmages. The 1953 Tennessee team had some hard hitters—people like McCord and Rotroff, Moose Barbish, Bob Fisher, and Mack Franklin—even though it wasn't a particularly good team. Upper classmen always enjoy putting special licks on freshmen. I guess that's only natural; somebody has to pay for what they went through when they were freshmen.

They certainly didn't hold anything back because I was the runt of the litter, and I took quite a pounding. But outside of Rotroff, who I was convinced would maim me if he could, I never felt any of them were really out to send me back to Huntland in a crate. It was just something we freshman backs had to endure, and we did. It was a part of paying our dues, and in the process we helped the team and learned something about holding up under adversity.

Our 1953 freshman team played only four games, and I missed the last two because of injuries. Ike Peel and Bunzy O'Neil were our coaches, and they both were very helpful to me. We had two units, a single wing team and a T formation team. Since I was the T quarterback on the scout squad, I didn't get to play tailback at all that year. It wasn't until spring practice between my freshman and sophomore seasons that I got a chance to see what I could do at the position that I felt was the natural one for me.

I had a great spring practice in 1954, making some long runs in scrimmage and getting big write-ups in the Knoxville papers. When I got loose on a ninety-yard touchdown that gave the Orange team a 20–14 win in the spring game, one of the sportswriters got carried away and compared my broken field running with the great Red Grange. I knew better, even then, but it felt good to know that I had made an impression.

Nevertheless, I knew I had a long way to go. I wasn't throwing the ball nearly as well as I needed to, and I did not know how to call the plays the way a college quarterback should. This was long before coaches started sending plays in from the sidelines. The quarterback called them in the huddle, and in the Tennessee system the tailback was the quarterback.

After spring practice, Coach Robinson asked me if I would mind being red-shirted that fall. I said I wouldn't mind, but actually I was delighted. I figured that ahead of me there were two good tailbacks, Jimmy Wade and Pat Oleskiak, as well as two pretty good backups in Bobby Brengle and T. L. Cloar. Although I would sit out a year, red-shirting would give me a chance to play a lot more later.

Meanwhile, I was much more concerned about my school work than about football, and for a practical reason. My scholarship was for four years, and it could be revoked only if I failed to maintain a 2.0 grade average or if I was suspended from school for some kind of disciplinary problem. I knew that I wouldn't be suspended because, although I wasn't any angel, I've always had a healthy respect for, or even fear of, authority. I was not going to do anything to cause the coaches to suspend me.

It was during this time that I met another of the great teachers who meant so much to me during my school years. Dr. Ira Nelson Chiles was my faculty advisor, but he became my friend and counselor as well. I was able to turn to Dr. Chiles in many matters, not just school work. He loved lapidary work and became an expert in stones and minerals, and he made me a ring of my birthstone, emerald, which I still wear.

Dr. Chiles died shortly after my return to Tennessee as a coach, and I visited him at the hospital during his last illness. He was a man of deep religious faith, and he told me that he knew he was going to Heaven. "When I get there I'm going to see some people I don't expect to see," he said. And with a twinkle in his eye he added, "And some of the people I expect to see probably won't be there!"

When I was a student, the university had a study hall for freshmen, and all of us had to attend it every night until we established at least a 2.0 grade average. I wanted to make good grades for two reasons: to make sure I kept that scholarship and to get out of study hall in the future. So I knuckled down on the books.

I wasn't exactly a social lion on campus as a freshman. I was so busy with football and school, I didn't have much time for social life. Also, I couldn't afford it, as fifteen dollars a month, which is what scholarship athletes got in those days for incidental expenses, wouldn't take you very far in Knoxville, even in the 1950s. I did get some show passes, though. Sometimes I would take Dorothy Holt, whom I had dated in high school, to the movies. The fifteen dollars a month, show passes, and football season tickets kept me going through most of my University of Tennessee days, although I did make some extra money as an advanced ROTC student when I was an upperclassman. I joined Sigma Chi fraternity the spring quarter of my freshman year and became more active socially after that. But during my freshman year, most nights you could find me at home in the East Stadium dorm.

✦10✦

Fast Start—Slow Finish

Coach Robinson had to abandon his plans to red-shirt me in my sophomore year. Early in fall practice two fullbacks were hurt, and he had to move Pat Oleksiak to fullback to back up Tom Tracy. So he decided to activate me. This was a disappointment to me as I figured I needed that year to grow and learn. At the same time, however, I was excited. The prospect of actually playing for the varsity was pretty heady wine.

I really didn't know whether or not I would get to play when we made the trip to Memphis our opening game with Mississippi State. Nevertheless, I knew for that I had better be ready just in case. In practice that week they had me alternating with Bobby Brengle as the second string tailback behind Jimmy Wade, so I knew there was a possibility I would play. As it turned out, I not only played, but I made the longest touchdown run of my entire Tennessee career.

It happened in the second quarter. We were on our nineteen-yard line when I called a 57-W, a weakside version of our spinner trap play where the tailback fakes the ball to the fullback and then takes off to the weak side. I broke loose and went eighty-one yards for a touchdown. If I were making a movie, I couldn't have dreamed up a wilder script than that. While I didn't score a touchdown the very first time I carried the ball in a college game, it was close enough to make some big news.

Not long after the run, I came out of the game and a photographer for the *Nashville Banner* asked the coaches for permission to pose me with two Vol cheerleaders—Donna Gardner and

Nancy Boone—on the sidelines and they gave him permission. I did what I was told to do, but there is no way I would ever let that happen on the Tennessee sidelines today.

We beat Mississippi State, 19–7. Unfortunately, the rest of the 1954 season didn't turn out as happily as that day, for the team or for me. We wound up with a 4–6 record, the first losing season for Tennessee since 1935; and Harvey Robinson and most of his staff were fired shortly after the last game.

Young Johnny Majors didn't turn out to be quite the whizz-bang that he was expected to be after his sensational debut!

For the first time since I had started playing football, injuries kept me off the field for a good portion of the season. I missed four games because of some piddling, nagging little injuries that were not very serious but still were bad enough that the team physician, Dr. Bob Brashear, and the trainer, Mickey O'Brien, wouldn't let me play. Their judgment was right. I had no business playing, but I hated sitting out a game.

I played a lot in the second game, which we lost to Duke, 7–6, at Durham. I got my first and only start against Alabama, at Shields-Watkins Field, a huge thrill for me because of the Tennessee–Alabama games I had seen there when I was in high school.

That day, however, belonged to Albert Elmore. It sure wasn't mine. Elmore, who alternated with Bart Starr at quarterback, had one of the greatest days a quarterback has ever had. He passed and ran us crazy. On our side of the field, I threw two or three interceptions and fouled up the works in general. We lost, 27–0, and I'm sure that hurt Coach Robinson's standing more than anything else that happened that year.

A sprained ankle kept me out of the next two games, and then I got to play some against Georgia Tech at Atlanta. The coaches had decided to use me when we got inside the ten-yard line, not because I was a strong runner but because I followed the guards well on the power plays. I scored the first touchdown in that game, but the next time we got close to the end zone I let the Tech student section get to me a little bit with all the noise. I was distracted and messed up the snap count. We drew a penalty and failed to score. Tech beat us 28–7.

By this time the Vols were sliding downhill pretty fast. I hurt a knee before the Kentucky game, taking a hard lick in practice, and missed the game. However, I played most of the second half against Vanderbilt at Nashville in the last game of the season, mostly because I talked Ralph Chancey, the backfield coach, into letting me run back the kickoff. Vanderbilt beat us, 26–0.

A few days later I was at Alumni gym watching the Vol basketball team play when it was announced that Coach Robinson had been fired.

People sometimes ask me about that 1954 season and about Harvey Robinson. I want to set my impressions straight. First, it should be made clear that Coach Robinson was both a complete gentleman and a great scholar of the game. I was just an underclassmen, and sophomore players and head coaches don't generally pal around a lot. However, I got to know him as a peer later when he was scouting for the Dallas Cowboys. I don't know of anybody who knew the game more thoroughly, especially offense, and as a person he was kind and compassionate in every way.

I suppose no coach ever suffered more from unfortunate timing. He not only had to succeed a legend, General Neyland, but he also took over at a time when the talent level was far below what it had been in the previous few years. On top of that, the rules had been changed after the 1952 season, and he was faced with the task of teaching young, inexperienced athletes how to play both offense and defense.

That got him in trouble on defense, where he installed a new "umbrella" formation that, frankly, had most of the players confused. I knew nothing about the thinking behind that move, but I have heard that he felt there wasn't time to teach the old wide tackle six, because the players had to spend half their practice time on offense.

At any rate, things got worse as the season went along. Winning and losing have a great effect on everybody connected with a football team, the coaches as well as the players, and morale sagged badly in the last half of the season. The players sensed the friction among the coaches. There was a lot of bitching and moaning, and sometimes an assistant would snap at Coach Robinson, and sometimes he would light into one of them.

I hated that, because I liked all the coaches. Farmer Johnson, who had recruited me, was one of my all-time favorite people.

He continued to give me encouragement even after he was no longer on the Tennessee staff. Ralph Chancey, Burr West, Chan Caldwell, and Al Hust were all as nice to me as they could be. I certainly wouldn't want to blame anyone for the failure of that season, because I have learned from experience that winning takes care of a lot of mistakes and losing magnifies them.

Harvey Robinson was a good coach who was in the wrong place at the wrong time. I realize he could not have refused the job, but I am glad I never have had to follow a legend.

I would much prefer to take over a program that is down, rather than to follow a successful coach, especially one who was still there looking over my shoulder as athletic director. Even if you didn't have much to work with, at least you would have the opportunity to do things your way.

·11·

Exit Tom the Bomb

When Bowden Wyatt took over as Tennessee's head football coach in January of 1955, everything changed. He was like someone with a new broom; he swept the place clean.

Since everyone had expected Coach Wyatt to be the next coach, I had watched his Arkansas team very closely on television when they played in the Cotton Bowl on New Year's Day. I was impressed with his version of the single wing offense. It was different from the style we had been using at Tennessee where we had leaned heavily on the buck lateral series and other finesse-type plays. Coach Wyatt's single wing was a basic, clean, offense that seemed to me to have a lot in common with the pure power game that General Neyland had used so effectively in the past. I was anxious to get out on the field and find out how it would work for us.

I had seen Coach Wyatt once earlier. He had visited the Tennessee practice field when I was a freshman, and all the players had been impressed with him. He was a big, handsome man with a commanding presence. My wife, Mary Lynn, has frequently said that he was the most handsome man she has ever seen (I've never had the nerve to ask her where I rank on her list).

There was no question that Coach Wyatt had the air of the natural leader about him. He took charge at Tennessee from the moment he made his first appearance on campus, when he attended the football banquet and made a fiery talk I'm sure was aimed at the team. It was the perfect thing to do, for he got us thinking in terms of our own pride and Tennessee's great tradition.

Next, he and his staff immediately put us on an off-season conditioning program that was quite advanced for the time. He stressed strength and endurance in his conditioning, using a lot of strenuous exercises like boxing and climbing peg boards to accomplish his goals. Those of us who survived the ordeal went into spring practice in much better shape than we ever had been. Several players simply quit. They packed up and left the campus either before spring training or during it. His approach to conditioning impressed me so much that when it became my time to become a head coach years later, I borrowed many of Coach Wyatt's ideas for my own program.

The coaching staff was superb. Dick Hitt, who headed the defense, was Coach Wyatt's right hand man. A tough, demanding coach, he was always fair with the players. Skeeter Bailey, who coached the linemen, was in charge of calisthenics. He loved to put us through our paces, but I never enjoyed that part of practice. George Cafego, one of the greatest of all the Tennessee All-Americans, coached the tailbacks and kickers. Jim McDonald, who had enjoyed great success as a high school coach in Ohio, was in charge of the linebackers. Leroy Pearce, a young assistant, had come with Coach Wyatt from Arkansas. Ralph Chancey and Bunzy O'Neil had been retained from the old Robinson staff.

Discipline was the byword on Coach Wyatt's teams. My buddy, Frank Kolinsky, found this out the hard way early in spring practice. He and two or three of his friends were standing on the sidewalk outside Ellis and Ernest drugstore one night after curfew when one of the coaches spotted them. The next day on the practice field Coach Wyatt told Dick Hitt, "We'd better get these people's attention. They don't seem to think we're serious." Two hours later Frank and his friends staggered off the practice field, after running who knows how many laps. Without a doubt they were aware that Wyatt was serious!

After seeing the price they paid for breaking training rules, I was careful not to break any of them. It wasn't long, however, before I felt the sting of one of the coaches' remarks. Shortly after the new staff took over, I was leaving the weight room one day when Leroy Pearce entered. "Who are you?" he asked.

"Majors," I replied.

"Oh, yeah. You're the one who can't tell orange from red."

He was referring to the Alabama game the previous year in which I had thrown two interceptions. At the time he said it I was upset, but once I got to know Coach Pearce I realized it was just his way of dealing with players. He hadn't been out of college long himself and had a lot to learn about handling people; later he became a highly respected end coach.

One of the most famous practice field incidents in Tennessee football history took place on the first day of spring practice in 1955. Tom "The Bomb" Tracy, a stocky little fullback with some of the best moves I have ever seen, was our best running back. To this day I don't think I have seen anyone who could run better laterally.

Tom was a marvel at the trap and spinner plays that required timing and balance, and he was a master of open field running. He reminded me a lot of Hugh McElhenny, the great running back for the San Francisco 49ers of that era. As an individual, however, Tom was a little unpredictable. He wore zoot suits and spade-toed shoes, and he wasn't particularly concerned with keeping training rules. I suppose that with his style, sooner or later there would have been a confrontation between Tom and Coach Wyatt, even if this particular incident had never taken place.

We scrimmaged on that first day, and on the second or third series of downs Tom went down with leg cramps. He had great legs with huge muscles, and he got cramps pretty often. He hollered "Mickey!" for our trainer, Mickey O'Brien, and everyone figured we would get a short break while Mickey worked on Tom's legs.

However, Coach Wyatt stepped right over Tom and yelled at the student manager, "Move the ball up five yards and give me another fullback!"

As soon as Coach Wyatt said that, a sophomore named Tommy Bronson ran out on the field. He didn't wait to be picked out of the crowd. From that day on, he stayed on the first team and became one of the best fullbacks Tennessee ever had. I've often thought back to that day on Lower Hudson Field, when one great fullback moved out and another great one moved in to take his place in just a matter of a few seconds.

Tracy was angry and started talking with some of the other players about how he was going to quit. By the time he got back to his room at the dorm that night, Skeeter Bailey and Leroy Pearce had packed up his gear in boxes, and that was the end of Tom Tracy as a Tennessee football player.

Looking back on it from now, I think the problem was mainly one of timing. Given a few weeks or months, Tom Tracy might have worked into the Wyatt program. He was a truly fine football player, and I've found that good football players rarely quit. Tom later became a standout pro player, first in the Canadian League under Chan Caldwell, one of Coach Robinson's old assistants, and then with Detroit in the NFL.

From a coach's standpoint, Wyatt's move seems a bit severe, but sometimes a coach has to be severe when building a program. The team has to come first, and the coach has to make it clear that being a star player will not win any favors. General MacArthur said, "The corps and the corps and the corps." With me it's, "The team and the team and the team."

Tommy Bronson became one of the best friends I have ever had. Some people have been kind enough to call our 1955 and 1956 backfield one of the best in Tennessee history. I don't know about that, but I have always felt we were about as close as any unit could be.

Bill Anderson took the wingback job away from my buddy Bob Hibbard. Bill, who was rangy and fast and a good blocker and pass receiver, later had a fine professional career with the Washington Redskins and the Green Bay Packers. Stockton Adkins, the fullback, was the blocking back. "Old reliable" as a blocker, he also was a fine pass receiver, which was important in Wyatt's offensive plans since he liked to dump off passes underneath the passing coverage to the blocking back. Stockton beat out Jimmy Beutel, the team captain, one of the few times a Tennessee captain has had a starting job taken away from him. I was the tailback.

If ever there has been a team-oriented football player, it was Tommy Bronson. Nobody ever loved to play more than Tommy did. He was one of those guys who would knock down the dressing room door to get out on the field. While he wasn't all that big physically and certainly wasn't very fast, he developed his skills and played very intelligently. Totally committed to the game and to the team, he was the kind of player that makes a team great.

And it all began with a leg cramp.

·12·

The Second Block

Playing for Bowden Wyatt made me feel right at home because he and my dad were very much alike in their approach to the game. Neither tolerated any nonsense, both emphasized the fundamentals, and both were builders.

Few people today realize what a great coach Bowden Wyatt was. In the space of six or seven years he won championships in three different conferences: the Big Sky, the Southwestern, and the Southeastern. I do not know of any other coach who has ever done that.

At Tennessee Coach Wyatt built a solid, disciplined single wing offense on one of General Neyland's old principles: "Make it sound, make it simple, and keep it consistent."

Wyatt never overcoached. On game days he would have short meetings with his tailbacks at breakfast, throwing little pop quizzes at us. "We're leading 7–6 in the second quarter, and it's third and three on our thirty-six-yard line. What play do you call?" We would come up with our answers, and he might say, "Not bad, but how about number so and so?" And on we would go.

Like all Tennessee football coaches of the Neyland era, Coach Wyatt always retained a basically conservative approach to the game. Without fail, the last thing he would say to me at the pregame meal was, "If you can't think of anything else to call, kick the damned ball!"

That was the Neyland philosophy, and it was 100 percent right in its day. We weren't nearly as interested in who had the football, as in where it was on the field. If we got it inside the twenty-five-yard line on our end of the field, we were apt to punt on third down rather than risk a turnover close to our own goal line.

The quick kick was a regular part of our repertoire, and it helped us win several games, including the classic victory over Georgia Tech in 1956. Once we moved into four-down territory, we were a pretty good bet to take it on in for a touchdown. At least, by the second half of the 1955 season we had grown into that kind of offensive team.

Today football teams can't follow the same kind of game plan to the extent that we followed it. Offenses have become so hard to stop that a team has to hold onto the ball as long as possible to keep it out of the other team's hands. It is much more important to maintain possession today than it was in the '50s, but today's coaches would do well to borrow from the old game now and then. The quick kick is still a great surprise weapon, and my philosophy of the complete kicking game is still pretty much what it was when I played at Tennessee.

We lost our first two games under Coach Wyatt. Mississippi State beat us 13–7 in the season opener. We did, however, have a small omen of things to come when I hit Buddy Cruze with a touchdown for our only score. Over the next two seasons, Buddy and I hooked up for several long gains and touchdowns, and his fine hands, and unbelievable ability to twist his body in the air and come down with the ball made me look good more than once.

We lost our second game, 21–0, to Duke and Sonny Jurgenson. Since both these games were at home, I'm sure many fans were beginning to wonder whether the coaching change had improved the situation or not. While the coaches and players were still learning to adapt to each other, it didn't take much longer to make some adjustments. Bill Anderson and Stockton Adkins were moved into the first team backfield, and Lon Herzbrun was shifted from fullback to guard.

Lon felt he was moved into the line as punishment. "I made a great block for John," he said, "and I was standing there admiring my handiwork when the coaches jumped all over me. They wanted me to run on downfield and look for somebody else to knock down!"

The second block was another trademark of Tennessee football. Legend has it that when Johnny Butler made his great touchdown run against Alabama in 1939, the blocking back, Ike Peel, made three separate blocks on the play.

After two losses, we jelled as a team. One of our two biggest wins in 1955 was over Alabama, 20–0, at Legion Field in Birmingham. I had a good day, which was a relief after my performance of the previous year, although I shanked two punts, something I never had done and never did again.

Bill Johnson, a sophmore who later became an All-American, picked up a new nickname in the Alabama game. He was lined up against a tough Alabama lineman named Nick Germanos, and Germanos "mashed" him around a few times that day. After that everybody started calling him "Geronimo," a nickname that has stuck to this day with his old teammates.

We tied Georgia Tech, 7–7, in 1955, in a grinding battle at Shields-Watkins Field. Since both teams were composed mostly of juniors and sophomores, it was sort of a preview of the great game played the following year. I played the entire game, and I've often wondered since then if I was the last Tennessee man to play a full sixty minutes.

I did have one embarrassing moment. We were at about our own thirty-five-yard line when I dropped the ball I was punting. I never did figure out what happened. Georgia Tech's rush wasn't very aggressive, and I faced little pressure. When the ball slipped through my hands, I felt so foolish and helpless. Fortunately we held Georgia Tech from scoring; so my big bobble didn't cost us any points.

The following week Tommy Bronson had one of those games every football player dreams of having. The University of Florida had overlooked him when he was a high school player and had not offered him a scholarship. Since he grew up in Gainesville, where the University is located, he had a point to prove; and he made it very well. I kept calling his number. He was hot; and we won the game, 20–0.

As we waited to board the train to Kentucky for the next-to-last game of the season, several of us players did a very stupid thing. We were to leave from the old Southern Railway station, and several of us decided it would be neat if we bought big hats and wore them when we got on the train. I have long since forgotten why we thought it would be cute, but we bought the hats, put them on, and paraded through the depot looking like fools.

I knew I had made a big mistake when I saw Coach Wyatt looking at me. He did not say a word; he just gave me a look that would have had me eating the hat gladly if I could have found some salt and pepper. It reminded me of the look my dad would give us when we fouled up back at Huntland High. Of course, the hat wasn't the issue; the problem was that we weren't approaching the game with the right attitude.

Kentucky beat us badly the next day, 23–0, and I learned two things. One was never to clown around before a football game. The other was never to overlook Kentucky. Nobody has to remind me of what can happen in that old rivalry. It was one of the most thorough whippings I remember Tennessee receiving.

It was a cold, drizzly, sleety kind of day, and Kentucky had a much larger team than we did. They seemed to get a lot better footing on the turf, too. Our small guards, Bill Johnson and Charley Coffey, were pushed, slipping and sliding, all over the field that day. In the first quarter I practically walked into the end zone from the one-yard line on the weakside number one play, but Bill had jumped offsides and the touchdown was nullified.

Johnson and Coffey were built very much alike. Both were small and compact, and both were great guards. Bill was quicker, but Charley was stronger; and they fussed at each other constantly. They called each other "Jughead," which was very misleading since both of them won awards at one time or another as the team's best scholar. Charley was very proud of his strength, so one night in the dorm some of us rigged up a trick to take some of the wind out of his sails. We took one of the pull-apart elastic flex devices that test your strength and had both of them try it. We gave it to Bill first, and he pulled it to its limit. Everybody started shouting, "Hey, look at Johnson!" Then we challenged Coffey, who said he knew he could do it if Johnson could. While he was talking, somebody tightened the stress on the apparatus; and when Charley took his turn, he couldn't budge it. For a long time we didn't tell Charley what we had done, and until we let him in on the joke it bothered him to think that Bill had beaten him.

We still had the Vanderbilt game to play after our fiasco at

Shirley Inman Majors as a senior at Englewood High School.

My brother Joe, age 1, and me, age 3.

My family when I was nine years old. *Front* (*l* to *r*): Joe Majors, age 7; Cap Lawson (cousin), age 2; Bill Majors, age 5; John Terrill Majors, age 9; Shirley Ann Majors, age 4; Larry Majors, age 3. *Back* (*l* to *r*): Grandmother Ella Sanders Majors; Great-aunt Nora Sanders Majors; Aunt Ann Majors; Uncle Owen Majors; Daddy; Mother.

Grandmother and Grandfather Bobo; *(bottom)* Elizabeth Bobo Majors; *(top)* Mary Frances Bobo Copeland.

My first day of school, September 15, 1941, age 6.

The Bubble Gum Gang (*l* to *r*): Bill Majors, John Terrill Majors, David "Chicken" Cunningham, Kenny Harrison, Joe Majors.

Left: My brother Bob, who was born when I was fourteen years old. *Right* (*l* to *r*): Larry, Shirley Ann, Bill, Joe, and me all lined up in a row.

The Majors clan in uniform and ready to go (*l* to *r*): Bob, Larry, Bill, Joe, me, and Daddy.

The 1952 Huntland High School championship team. *Front* (*l* to *r*): Harold Limbaugh, Joe Earl Carwell, Paul Isbell, Hulen Watson, Ralph Ayres, Ben Sutton, Wayne "Duck" Williams. *Back* (*l* or *r*): Leon Steele, Donald Schultz, W. A. "Slats" McCreeless, John Majors.

My graduation photo from Huntland High School, 1953.

Clowning around with W. R. "Slats" McCreeless in front of Huntland High.

Larry, Bill, Daddy and Bob watching me play on Shields-Watkins Field in Knoxville.

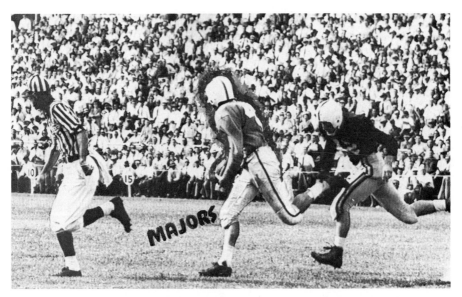

En route to an eighty-one-yard touchdown against Mississippi State in my first varsity game at Tennessee.

Posing on sideline after my long run against Mississippi State with (*l* to *r*) Donna Gardner and Nancy Boone.

The Majors family in 1956.
Front (*l* to *r*): Dad, me, Mom.
Back (*l* to *r*): Shirley Ann,
Joe, Bill, Larry, Bob.

In New Orleans on Saturday, December 29, 1956, prior to the Sugar Bowl game (*l* to *r*): John Majors, Bob Gleaves,
Bill Johnson.

Preparing to board the train with the team (*l* to *r*): John Majors, John Gordy, General Neyland, Buddy Cruze.

Action against Kentucky in 1956. Notice all the blockers in perfect position and Buddy Cruze open for a pass downfield in the event Lou Michaels heads off the run.

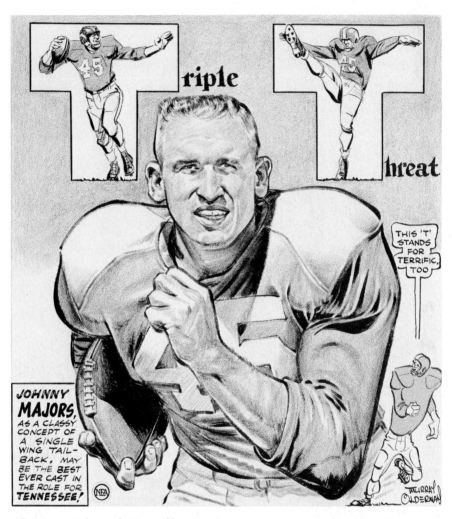

A flattering poster about me by Murray Olderman.

Making an appearance at the Knoxville Junior Chamber of Commerce in 1956 (*l* to *r*): John Gordy, Coach Bowden Wyatt, and me.

Celebrating a perfect season and a victory over Vanderbilt at the completion of our 1956 schedule, with John Gordy (*l*) and Buddy Cruze (*r*).

At the Birmingham Touchdown Club in 1956 for the Southeastern Conference Back of the Year Award. Norman Downey *(m)* was program chairman, and Lou Michaels of Kentucky *(r)* was Lineman of the Year.

With my number one admirer, my brother Bob, when I received the Southeastern Conference Player of the Year Award for the second time in 1956. Bob carried around the award all evening before we were asked to pose for the cameras.

The 1956 Colliers All-America Team on the Ed Sullivan Show. *Front* (*l* to *r*): Ron Kramer, Michigan; John White, Oregon State; Jim Parker, Ohio State; Bill Glass, Baylor; Lou Michaels, Kentucky; Joe Walton, Pittsburgh. *Back* (*l* to *r*): Johnny Majors, Tennessee; John Brodie, Standford; Jimmy Brown, Syracuse.

At the first Fellowship of Christian Athletes meeting in Tennessee, 1957.

Coaching the Tennessee freshman backs in 1958 (*l* to *r*): Coach John Majors, Jere Disney, Glenn Glass, Pat Augustine, Dave Shields.

The University of Tennessee freshman team coaching staff, 1957 (*l* to *r*): Hal Bridges, Edd Cantrell, Bobby Proctor, John Majors, Bob Neyland, Jr.

On our honeymoon Mary Lynn covered up my legs and named me Pigmy.

Right: On the beach in Florida with my bride, Mary Lynn.

The Majors family portrait, 1959. *Front* (*l* to *r*): Bobby, Shirley Ann, Daddy, Mother, Mary Lynn. *Back* (*l* to *r*): Larry, Joe, Bill, me.

The Mississippi State coaching staff, 1961. *Front* (*l* to *r*): Paul Davis, Wade Walker, Ken Donahue. *Back* (*l* to *r*): John Majors, J. P. Patrick, Henry Lee Parker, Jim Champion, Dave Owens.

The Arkansas coaching staff, 1966. *Front* (*l* to *r*): John Majors, Jim McKenzie, Frank Broyles, Wilson Matthews, Bill Pace. *Back* (*l* to *r*): Steed White, Jack Davis, Barry Switzer, Mervin Johnson, Lou Ferrel.

Kentucky. Vandy was an outstanding team that season, one of the best that I played against while I was at Tennessee. They had a 7–2 record going into the game, and they supposedly were in line for the Sugar Bowl. I don't like to admit it even at this late date, but they probably were a better team than we were that year. They had some truly standout players, like Don Orr at quarterback, Phil King and Charlie Horton as running backs, and Art Demos in the line.

We were out to make up for the bad beating we had taken at Nashville the previous year, and we played a little beyond our abilities. They stopped our running game, but we scored three touchdowns on passes to win, 20–14. I threw to Buddy Cruze for two of them, but the game-winner was a pass in the fourth quarter from Al Carter to Bill Anderson on a deep post pattern.

The crowd was one of the most exuberant I can remember. My dad sat in the section just behind the bench and came leaping across the fence onto the field after the game.

Following the game we "turned down" an invitation to play in the Gator Bowl. Actually, we never got to vote. Coach Wyatt simply told us we were not going. He later told us that he refused the bid because Auburn was the opponent, and since we were to open the 1956 season against them he didn't want to give them an advance look at the single wing.

So that's how Tennessee helped Vanderbilt go to the Gator Bowl after the 1955 season. Vandy played a good game and beat Auburn in Jacksonville.

✦13✦

The Vols Come of Age

We knew we had a chance to win the conference championship as we went into the 1956 season. We even dreamed of winning the national championship. We had had good spring and fall practices, we were experienced, and we were confident.

I was confident I could be an improved player in '56, even though I had made the All-Southeastern Conference team and had been picked the most valuable player in the conference as a junior. I had developed the "feel" of calling the plays, and I believed I could carry out Coach Wyatt's game plan even though there was very little contact between us once the game began. We played both ways then—offense and defense—and there was no opportunity to get a refresher course from the coaches while another unit was on the field.

The strategy of quarterbacking, as opposed to the physical task, is still a very important part of any football team's success. Even today it is important, although plays usually are sent in for every play. While the modern quarterback still has to know when to check to an alternate play and when not to do so, he doesn't have the total responsibility that quarterbacks had in years past.

I worked very hard to train myself to think along the same lines as Coach Wyatt and his staff. One of the nicest things he ever said about me was that I was "a coach on the field." Dick Hitt used to sit in a booth in the press box during the games and make notes; then he would help us with advice at half time. During one of our games in my senior year, Dick yelled out, "Run the option, Johnny!" Of course I couldn't hear him, but on the next play I ran the option and scored a touchdown.

In the first quarter of our 1956 opener against Auburn at Birmingham, I crossed up the coaches with a play they didn't want. We had fourth and one at about the Auburn thirty-five. I later learned that Coach Wyatt was hollering, "Kick it, Johnny!" as loud as he could. I called the weakside option one play, rolled out to the left, and started to run. Then I spotted Buddy Cruze alone in the end zone and hit him for a touchdown. Coach Wyatt didn't fuss at me, but I've often wondered what he would have said if the pass had been incomplete.

Our play was machinelike against Auburn, and we beat them, 35–7. I still have a picture that ran in one of the Knoxville newspapers, showing our team at a moment of almost perfect execution. It was the tailback wedge play, and I scored a touchdown on it. The memorable thing about the picture was that it showed every one of the other ten players stepping in unison as they made their blocks. It was like looking at a military unit on the parade ground. I doubt very much if you ever would see such perfect execution in today's game, because few plays now call for the kind of precision that the old single wing demanded.

The following Saturday I had what probably was the greatest half of my career. We beat Duke, 33–20. As best I can remember, I rushed for over 100 yards, threw well, and scored a couple of touchdowns; those were big numbers back then. However, I couldn't add anything to them in the second half because I was out of action with the worst injury I ever suffered.

Late in the second quarter I called a third down pass play and had to scramble out of the pocket. I made about thirty yards on the play, carrying the ball inside the Duke ten. A big lineman tackled me from the blind side, and I felt my right shoulder come apart under the blow. Mickey O'Brien, the team trainer, ran out on the field and asked me if I wanted to come out, and I shook him off. I ran the next play to the one, then gave the ball to Tommy Bronson for the touchdown.

The injury turned out to be a third degree shoulder separation. I still have a deep indentation there, and our present Tennessee trainer, Tim Kerin, tells me that today that injury would knock a player out for an entire season. I guess I was lucky that modern sports medicine hadn't arrived as I certainly didn't want to miss the rest of the 1956 season.

Nevertheless, I did miss the Chattanooga game the next week. Then Mickey rigged up a big pad about three or four inches thick for me to wear, and I was able to return for the Alabama game two weeks later. I wore the pad the rest of the season, and I didn't practice very much after that. The shoulder was so stiff I could hardly lift my arm. I would limber it up on Thursday and Friday, and by Saturday I could use it again.

Mickey did an amazing job with me, but then he was a legend to three generations of Vols. He came to Tennessee in 1938, just in time to play a part in the great seasons of the late '30s and early '40s, and he stayed on under coaches Robinson, Wyatt, Jim McDonald, Doug Dickey, and Bill Battle before retiring in the early '70s. One of the great football trainers of all time, he was one of the first inducted into the Football Hall of Fame.

Tennessee players remember Mickey mostly as a friend. He was funny without meaning to be funny. He had a halting speech pattern, and sometimes it took him a long time to say what he wanted to say. There always was at least one guy on every Tennessee team who could do a Mickey O'Brien impression. They say that Al Rotella, back in the '40s, was the best of them.

Mickey always had plenty of advice to offer. Once during my freshman year he gave me advice that came too late to help me. During a scrimmage in my freshman year, I got tackled and extended my free hand to cushion the blow as I struck the ground, dislocating the elbow. I had never felt such excruciating pain, and the injury kept me out of the last four or five weeks of my freshman season. As he led me off the field, Mickey said, "Kid" (he always called his players "kid"), let me give you some advice. Don't ever put your hand down to break your fall." I wished he had told me that a little sooner.

I returned for the Alabama game. I didn't want to miss that one. Even though this was not a great Alabama team, they still were Alabama and we still were Tennessee. Coach Wyatt, who had played in some of the greatest games of this rivalry, wasn't about to let us be complacent. "I hate those S.O.B.'s," he'd say. "They broke my jaw one year."

We beat Alabama, 24–0, at home, getting a lot of mileage out of one of our standby plays. In it the tailback would get the ball and stand up straight while the fullback cleared the area. Then the tailback would take off on an option run. Almost always we had run the play to the weak side, but in this game I ran it to the strong side. The Alabama linebackers got caught moving in the wrong direction, and I went forty-four yards for a touchdown.

The following Saturday against Maryland, I was hurt again. Their big All-American lineman, Mike Sandusky, hit me square and hard, and I went out with an injured rib. That kept me out of the North Carolina game the next week, except for one play. The coaches put me in with the second team in the second half, and the crowd gave me a nice ovation. Their safety was pulled in close, and I quick-kicked the ball to their ten-yard line.

Ed Wyatt, Coach Wyatt's brother, was on the sidelines that day, and I remember him asking, "Bowden, why did you put Majors in for just one play?"

Coach Wyatt answered, "I was making certain that he gets in enough quarters to earn a letter."

Beating both Maryland and North Carolina handily set the stage for the biggest game of the season, and the biggest of my career. It took place at Grant Field in Atlanta against Georgia Tech on November tenth.

·14·

A Game to Remember

Few college football games have lived as long in memory as the Tennessee–Georgia Tech game of 1956. It was a classic matchup of two teams that played the old field position, don't-beat-yourself style of football. Both played it about as well as it ever has been played.

Both coaches, Bowden Wyatt of Tennessee and Bobby Dodd of Georgia Tech, were protegés of General Neyland. They both had learned their lessons well. We knew this game would be played as close to the vest as it could be played and that one break—a fumble, an interception, a blocked kick, or a kick runback—could mean the difference between winning and losing.

The buildup and pregame excitement were something else. Both teams had perfect records. Georgia Tech was ranked number two in the nation, and we were ranked number three. Tickets were being sold at outrageous prices, and I'll have to admit that I did a little enterprising on the side and came out pretty well. I had figured that this would be the game of the year ever since our game the previous season, so during the summer I had purchased several extra tickets. I sold them for one hundred dollars each. At that time the NCAA had no rule against players doing this. It was the only time during my four years at Tennessee that I had any money worth mentioning.

There was an overflow crowd at Grant Field that day, and not long before the kickoff some fans who couldn't get tickets crashed the north gate. Despite the diversions, we approached the game very businesslike and did not get caught up in the emotion. We knew that any mistake we made would be magnified and that we would have to be on our toes for every play.

From the start the emphasis was on kicking. Tech drove down to our twenty-eight-yard line early in the game, and on fourth down and three they punted the ball dead inside our ten. Coach Dodd was second-guessed for not going for the first down, but I've always liked Coach Wyatt's comment when he heard of it. He said, "Hell, he wouldn't have made it!"

It was our turn to move the ball. On third down they played us to quick kick, and I ran to the weak side and picked up the first down. Then I quick-kicked! The ball went sixty-nine yards and rolled dead inside their fifteen.

In the battle for field position, we had swapped ends of the field in one dramatic moment. Coach Dodd later said that it was the best call ever made against him, and that made me awfully proud. I know it was the best call I ever made.

However, it only gave us a temporary upper hand. It was still back and forth, touch and go, and it remained that way throughout the game. Georgia Tech had two sets of great running backs, and they were dangerous anywhere on the field. On one play George Volkert almost broke loose two or three times, and one of those times he would have slipped a tackle on me but someone else hit him just in time.

My quick kick was only the first of several big kicking plays. I had a pooch kick that turned sideways and died on the Tech six-inch line. Bobby Gordon, our second unit tailback, who was one of the strongest punters I ever saw, boomed one seventy-six yards from deep punt formation. And Tech set us back once with a great quick kick.

The game's only score came early in the third quarter. We had the ball at about midfield, moving toward the north goal. I set up the big play with another one called "weak end outside." From formation left, I faked a draw to the fullback, Bronson, and threw a twelve- or fifteen-yard pass to Buddy Cruze who was cutting outside from the right. On the next snap we ran what looked like the same play, except that Buddy cut inside this time. The Tech safety man, Wade Mitchell, overran Cruze and bumped into his own defensive halfback, causing both of them to fall.

Buddy caught the ball and took off for the goal line. He was tackled before he could score, and I had no doubt at all about which play to call for the last yard. I gave it to the best wedge runner who ever played the game, Tommy Bronson, and he slammed it into the end zone. Bob Smithers missed the extra point, and we knew that if Tech scored we probably would lose. The rest of the game seemed to last for hours, but our line, which played a magnificent game, stopped them.

Late in the game, one of our reserve blocking backs, Bill Bennett, suffered a broken leg. Mickey O'Brien and Dr. Brashear made him as comfortable as they could, and he was propped up near the team bench when the game ended. The excitement was so great that everybody just took off, first to the middle of the field and then to the dressing room, that is everybody except poor old Bill. He couldn't move, and it was a long time before someone finally remembered him and brought him into the dressing room.

It was a jubilant Tennessee team and a jubilant Tennessee crowd that made its way back through midtown Atlanta after the game. The traffic was so thick we were late, and they had to delay the train.

Back in Knoxville we had another celebration when the Associated Press ranked Tennessee number one early the following week.

·15·

Lou Michaels

So much has been made of the Georgia Tech game in 1956 that some people seem to think that was the only real challenge Tennessee faced that season. Actually, we probably came closer to defeat against Kentucky than anybody else.

The Wildcats had beaten us badly at Lexington in 1955, and we knew that any team that had Lou Michaels playing for it meant trouble. Michaels was a one-man army, the meanest, toughest football player I ever faced. And I know a lot of others who would agree with me.

Officially, Lou was a tackle. But he was just as likely to line up outside the end or on the center's nose. He was like an 800-pound grizzly bear that sleeps wherever it wishes; he played wherever he wanted. And he hated Tennessee with a burning passion.

We had our own great tackle, John Gordy, a senior and the captain of the team. John weighed about 230 pounds, the only man in the lineup over 210. He was a quick, natural athlete and a superb football player.

John's parents and mine were friends, and before the game Mrs. Gordy said to my mother, "Mrs. Majors, John has never scored a touchdown in all the time has has been playing football. I wish he could somehow score just one before he's through playing."

We took the opening kickoff and marched straight downfield on a sixteen-play drive that used up twelve minutes. I made sure I knew where Michaels was lined up on every play and sent the ball the opposite direction. Inside the ten and lined up in single wing right, I called the weakside off-tackle play. Gordy, the strong side tackle, was supposed to clear out the tackle opposite him—Michaels—with a brush block. I later told him he did a great job of it; he couldn't have brushed Michaels much more lightly.

By the time I reached the weakside tackle hole, Michaels was there waiting for me. I made a fundamental mistake by not switching the ball to the arm opposite Michaels, as I had been taught. He hit me, and the football squirted up in the air. Who else but John Gordy was there to catch it! John grabbed the ball and took it straight into the end zone before anybody knew what had happened. John had his touchdown, and we had a 6–0 lead.

Kentucky scored a touchdown of its own, and with Michaels shutting down our running game, they led us 7-6 midway through the fourth quarter. To make matters worse, we were backed up inside our ten-yard line. The crowd at Shields-Watkins Field was getting a little edgy; it looked as if our perfect record was about to go down the drain to the same rival that had spoiled so many Tennessee seasons in the past. Then we got a break.

I hit what may have been my best kick ever from deep punt formation, and it sailed over the head of the Kentucky safety man, Billy Mitchell. Once Mitchell got his hands on the ball, he reversed his field and lost more yardage; they also had a clipping penalty tacked on top of that. Then Kentucky started its own drive; but they fumbled, and we recovered the ball at midfield.

The momentum had swung our way. We drove the ball downfield quickly, and I scored on the weakside "one" option play, somersaulting into the end zone. Kentucky fumbled again, and I made two twenty-two-yard runs off weakside tackle. The last one was for another touchdown, and we won the game, 20–7.

Lou Michaels and I had been selected to the *Collier's* All-American football team that was to appear on the Ed Sullivan television show the following night in New York. A taxi was to pick us up at the Tennessee dressing room after the game and take us to the airport to catch the flight to New York. I had a lot of visitors after the game, so I asked my roommate, Bob

Gleaves, to find Michaels and ask him to come on up to our room at the dorm and wait for me.

Bob came back in a few minutes looking pretty pale. He said, "You may be in for a tough night." Michaels had told him that he hated Tennessee and that under no circumstances would he come inside the Tennessee football dorm.

When I went out to meet him, I said, "Hello, Lou."

No answer.

I tried to break the ice two or three more times during the ride to the airport. Still no answer.

The plane wasn't crowded. Lou sat down first. I didn't want to sit with him; but I was afraid it might make him mad if I didn't. So I moved in beside him. He didn't speak until we were over Washington, D.C.

Then he said, "I hope you and Gordy and Cruze play pro football because that will give me a chance to get even with you. You were lucky today, but I'll be waiting for you!"

The next thing he said was, "I can't wait till Tennessee comes to Lexington next year. They'll never forget Kentucky!"

He turned out to be a prophet. My buddies on the 1957 Tennessee team have told me about that game many times. Kentucky won it, 20–6, or maybe I should say Michaels won it. He opened the game by kicking off, and tackling the receiver Bobby Gordon, my successor at tailback, knocking the ball loose, and then recovering it to set up a touchdown. A few plays later he blocked a punt and recovered it in the end zone for a second touchdown.

Bill Johnson, who was an All-American guard that year, told me that all game long Michaels kept looking for him. He'd yell, "Where's Johnson?" and Bill says he would scrunch down as low as he could to escape notice. During the game Michaels splintered Johnson's face mask and split his face open from his lower lip to his chin.

Michaels was ferocious. Lonnie Herzbrun claims that Jim Smelcher, Tennessee's biggest tackle, once came back to the huddle looking out through the earhole of his helmet. Lonnie himself was victimized when Michaels hit him so hard with a forearm that it burst the laces on his shoulder pads. Lonnie had to leave the game while the managers looked for replacement laces. One of the substitutes kindly offered Lonnie his laces. "No thanks," said Lonnie. "I'll just wait."

So this was the guy I was paired with on the trip to New York. I weighed about 165 pounds, and he weighed about 240. I kept thinking how lovely it was going to be to get to the hotel and the sanctuary of my room.

The *Collier's* people had booked us in at the Lexington Hotel. When I got to the desk, the clerk said, "Mr. Majors, we have you in the same room with Mr. Michaels."

I didn't sleep much that night. Our room was on the eleventh floor, and I kept thinking how easy it would be for Lou to pick me up and throw me out of the window.

The next morning, Sunday, we met the rest of the All-American team, fellows like Jim Brown of Syracuse, Tommy McDonald of Oklahoma, John Brodie of Stanford, Joe Walton of Pittsburgh, Ron Kramer of Michigan, and Ohio State's great guard, Jim Parker. Some of them asked me about the Tennessee-Kentucky game, and I told them about the strange play in which Gordy scored his touchdown. Lou stood some distance away, glowering as usual. When Jim Parker heard the story about Gordy, he yelled out so everybody could hear him, "Hey, fellows, did you hear about Tennessee beating Kentucky on the old tackle pitchout play?" That didn't make things go any smoother between Michaels and me, and I was glad when I was safely out of New York.

Lou Michaels went on to be a great defensive lineman in the National Football League, but I didn't see him again until the day in 1975 at Birmingham, Alabama, when he and I both were picked on the twenty-five-year All-Southeastern Conference team by the *Birmingham News*. I had been talking with some of the sports writers in the hotel lobby. In fact, I had just finished telling them about Lou Michaels and the 1956 Tennessee-Kentucky game when I ran into him at the social hour. "Hello, Lou," I said.

He replied, "You were lucky!"

Later that night, Lou and Bob Gain and I got together at Pat James' restaurant for a couple of hours after the ceremonies. We had a great time, and I began to feel that maybe the relationship was reaching somewhat better terms.

I was coaching at Pittsburgh then. During the 1976 season I

ran across a feature in the *NCAA News* entitled, "Where Is Lou Michaels Now?" He was running his own bar in Swoyerville, Pennsylvania, and working as coach and athletic director at a prison on the side. The writer asked him if he still followed his old teams—Kentucky, the Steelers, Packers, and Colts. His answer was, "No, I keep up with the Pittsburgh Panthers and my old friend, John Majors!"

For the first time in twenty years I was relaxed when I thought of Lou Michaels.

My Pittsburgh team beat Penn State in the final game that season to finish 11–0, and there already was talk in public that I might go back to Tennessee. After the game, I was standing on a table in the dressing room talking with the press, when suddenly Lou came in and climbed up on the table with me. He didn't bother to say hello. He just said, "You had better not go to Tennessee!"

·16·

Burning the Biscuits

We beat a good Vanderbilt team in Nashville, 27–7, to nail down our perfect season and a Sugar Bowl bid. On an emotional high and anxious to win the Southeastern Conference championship, we played a solid game. I made one of the most enjoyable touchdown runs of my career on a weak side play where I cut back against the flow of the play, made three or four players miss me, and then leaped the last two yards over two defenders into the end zone. That was a particularly rewarding moment for me because Nashville was close to Lynchburg and Huntland, and a lot of my old friends were on hand. Also, in my previous appearance there, two years earlier, Vanderbilt had beaten us badly.

The players on that championship team have meant so much to me through the years. As a coach, I have since discovered that championship teams have something going for them that can't be measured in size, speed, and physical ability. They have pride, they're unselfish, and they are very close.

There is no camaraderie anywhere quite like that on a football team, especially on a winning team. Looking back, that means even more to me than the games we won. We weren't just teammates; we were good friends, and we still are. The University of Tennessee brought in football players from all over the nation, and we became a melting pot of sorts. Small town boys from Tennessee had to pick up the jargon and lingo of the big city dudes from the north and east. I learned very quickly about the boys from the steel and mill towns of Pennsylvania; it was a lesson that helped me later when I coached at Pittsburgh. They were from close-knit, blue collar families, and they had great qualities of loyalty and fearlessness. During one practice session in my freshman year, Ike Peel had us line up and make head-on tackles at full speed. Bob Hibbard of Midland, Pennsylvania, couldn't find a helmet that fit him; but he got in line anyway, bareheaded. That's how much he wanted to play and how brave he was.

We all did a lot of kidding, of course. Frank Kolinsky, who came from the Pittsburgh area and stayed on in Knoxville after his playing days, insists I rode into Knoxville from Huntland on a mule, barefooted and dressed in overalls. I took Frank home to Huntland with me for weekends a couple of times my freshman year, and he and I hitchhiked to Pittsburgh to visit his family during spring break.

I didn't know what kind of weather to expect, but Frank said it always was warm in Pittsburgh in the spring, so I wore my freshman numeral sweater. By the time we reached West Virginia, we were in the middle of the biggest snowstorm in twenty years, and I almost froze to death trying to hitchhike my way. The Kolinskys made me feel like a part of the family, and I became addicted to some of those delicious Polish dishes I hadn't even known about just days earlier. Years later when I flew from Iowa into Pittsburgh to take the coaching job there, Mrs. Kolinsky was at the airport to meet me.

We had great fun with the Yankees in our midst. On the bus we took to Kentucky for our freshman game in 1953, we went past a big barn that had tobacco hanging down its sides. This was no big deal to us Tennessee boys, but Lon Herzbrun, from Washington, D.C., pointed to the barn and said, "Man, look at those foxes!"

We never let him forget that one!

My roommate, Bob Gleaves, and Bill Johnson were two of my closest friends during college days. We belonged to the same fraternity, Sigma Chi. They were pretty good friends to have because they were almost the only guys on the squad who had their own cars. I was able to ride with them on dates, and sometimes one of them would let me borrow his car.

John Gordy was another good friend, but I had to steer clear of him when he was in a frisky mood. He got a big kick out of bullying me, and he would threaten to hold me out of the third story window at the dorm. That old trick had been pulled a number of times in the old East Stadium dorm, and I was determined that it wasn't going to happen to me.

None of us had much money, but most of the players from the 1956 team have done well in later life. Buddy Cruze owns his own computer business. Edd Cantrell has been a coach, teacher, and school administrator. John Gordy had a good NFL career and now is the president of a corporation. Roger Urbano is in the trucking business. Charley Coffey was a major college head coach and now owns his own trucking company. Bill Johnson is president of the First National Bank of Sparta, Tennessee, his hometown, and a member of the University of Tennessee Board of Trustees. Bruce Burnham is in the real estate business in Columbus, Ohio. Carl Smith is a horse trainer. Tommy Bronson is a highly successful business executive; the *Wall Street Journal* ran a page one story on him not too long ago. Charlie Rader, one of the most brilliant men I've ever known, is a top executive with Monsanto Chemical Company. Bob Gleaves owns an educational publishing and tutoring business in Nashville. Stockton Adkins is in financial planning in West Tennessee. Bill Anderson is a successful insurance agent, as well as a part-time sportscaster. Bob Hibbard is in the furniture manufacturing business in Knoxville. Our center, Bubba Howe, is now a longtime Memphis businessman. And nobody does more worthwhile work than Frank Kolinsky, who runs a halfway house in Knoxville for people who need help.

These were some of the 1956 Tennessee Vols who traveled to New Orleans for the Sugar Bowl game with Baylor on January 1, 1957. We were a good team and a happy team, but that was not to be our day. Baylor was a strong, tough, physical team, and they won the game, 13–7.

We were very disappointed to lose, but the outcome of the game almost became a secondary issue because of an incident on the field. We were leading 7–6 in the third quarter when a Baylor player named Larry Hickman kicked Bruce Burnham, one of our guards, in the head. Bruce was scramble blocking on the play and had hit one man and had lunged after another when Hickman kicked him as he lay on the ground.

That was the most frightening thing I have ever seen on a football field. Bruce went into convulsions, and we all thought he was dying. I had seen players knocked out cold and had been knocked out once myself in a freshman scrimmage, but this was much, much worse. The game was stopped for what seemed like thirty minutes or more, although it probably was more like ten or fifteen. I thought we were beginning to control the game at that point, but after Bruce's injury we just could not get it going again.

My fumble on a punt return set up Baylor's winning score. The "rule" for punt receivers is not to field one inside the ten yard line, but sometimes it is hard to be sure exactly where you are when you're concentrating on catching the ball. I drifted back to about the nine and caught the ball. At about the fifteen-yard line I was hit and fumbled. Baylor recovered and soon scored the winning touchdown.

That was the bad news. The good news was that Bruce was not as seriously injured as we had feared. When I first saw my mother outside the dressing room, we didn't even talk about the game. I just said, "Mother, Bruce is going to be okay."

After the game, the news people kept asking me about what caused the fumble. I was feeling pretty awful because I had let the team down. I didn't want to talk with anyone about it, and told them so. My mother later helped me put things in their proper perspective. "Everybody burns the biscuits once in a while," she said.

I sat in the back of the team bus on the ride into New Orleans for our postgame dinner. Coach Wyatt came back and sat beside me. "Johnny, go to the party and have a good time," he said. "You and the team did a great job for us this season, and we appreciate it. Now put what happened today behind you."

We all have our bad days, and I've had my share as a player and as a coach. I've found I am better off when I can laugh them off later. Despite its tragedies, life is basically a comedy. It's well to remember that in the dark moments.

In the month following the game, I made three public appearances on successive Saturdays in Upper East Tennessee. I signed autographs and talked to fans. At Kingsport a gentleman came up to me with a little girl about one year old. He wanted to talk with some friends, and I asked him if I could hold his little girl while he was gone.

The next week I got a letter from him. He wrote that when he left me to visit with his friends, one of them asked, "Who's that holding your little girl?"

"That's Johnny Majors," he answered.

"Johnny Majors?" said the friend. "Aren't you afraid he'll drop her?"

·17·

Peahead—The One and Only

Few people remember my professional football career, I imagine. It was an easy thing to forget.

I played for the Montreal Alouettes in the Canadian Football League in 1957 under one of the legendary football coaches of all time, Clyde "Peahead" Walker. Even though it was a brief part of my life, I look back on it as an enjoyable experience.

Before I left Knoxville for Montreal that June, I had a duty to perform that I felt I owed to some people who had been extremely nice to me. During my junior and senior seasons I had received mail from all over the country, mostly from kids. However, I had been so busy with football, school, and my other commitments that I had not had, or maybe taken, the time to respond to them. So before I headed to Montreal I asked Gus Manning, who at that time was the sports information director, to collect all the pictures of me he could find. I then sat down and wrote each of those people a thank-you note and sent them an autographed picture.

It was one of the best investments of my time I've ever made, because I have been repaid for it over and over. I don't know how many times people have come up to me since then to tell me they got a picture. Shortly after I became head coach at Iowa State, a young man introduced himself to me and said, "Thanks for the picture. It was two years late getting there, but I got it."

I had won several personal honors while I was at Tennessee. I'd be lying if I said they weren't important to me. I was All-Southeastern Conference twice, was named Player of the Year in the Southeastern Conference twice by the *Nashville Banner*, and was picked on just about all the All-American teams. Some of my teammates teased me about these awards, especially the first All-SEC award. After I received it, everytime I walked into a room or came onto the practice field, Johnson or Bronson would yell, "Here comes the MVP of the SEC!" Sometimes they would continue chanting it—"MVP of the SEC! MVP of the SEC!"

In my senior year I was the runner-up to Paul Hornung of Notre Dame for the Heisman Trophy. Some Tennessee fans were furious about that. We had had a 10–0 season and Notre Dame was 2–8; so they felt it was unfair. The way I look at it, a great football player won the award. To tell the truth, I didn't expect to win it with players like Jim Brown, Tommy McDonald, and Ron Kramer in the running. There's nothing wrong with second place in that group.

Along with my teammate Buddy Cruze, I made a second trip to New York to appear on the Perry Como TV show with the *Look* All-American team. The show's format was for Como to introduce each player to the audience. Then after the audience's applause died down, he would introduce the next player. When my turn came, he said, "And you're about my size."

Without thinking I said, "Yeah, but I can't sing." He got a big kick out of that, and the next year they began the tradition of writing some one-liners for the players.

Without even waiting for the National Football League draft, I signed with the Alouettes. They made me an offer that may not sound like much now, but in 1957 it looked like a fortune to a small town Tennessee boy. During my senior year at Tennessee, I had interviewed for a job with Clinton Campbell, who owned a Knoxville insurance business. He asked me how much money I aspired to make, and I answered, "Ten thousand dollars a year." Well, I got ten thousand from the Montreal club, plus a bonus of one thousand for signing. And I felt like a millionaire.

Figuring first things first, I bought the first car I ever owned from Lon Varnell, who was the basketball coach at Sewanee and a good friend of my dad's, now a successful show business promoter. The car was a black '57 Bel Air Chevrolet coupe with silver streaks on the fin tail, a white top, and red and black upholstery. I figured I was the coolest cat in town once I got behind the wheel of that little beauty.

I also was able to start paying off a fraternity debt to Sigma Chi. When I had joined the fraternity, I was under the impression that I was getting a free ride. That was a misunderstanding, and I ended up owing Sigma Chi several hundred dollars. I was delighted to be able to pay my bill. The good times I had had at the frat house certainly were worth more than the size of my bill, and I always have felt better when I owe no one any money.

At Montreal I shared an apartment with four of my teammates—Joel Wells and Bill Hudson from Clemson, Buddy Frick from South Carolina, and Ed Houring from Maryland. We were young guys making more money than we ever thought possible, and we had a ball.

Montreal was a good football town. Of course, hockey was the number one sport, but the Alouettes had just come off two or three straight runnerup finishes for the Gray Cup championship. We were not that good during the season I was there, but the interest was still high.

I started my first professional game as a rookie at offensive halfback and defensive safety. I didn't field punts on defense, because there was no fair catch rule in Canadian football and Peahead Walker always used a Canadian player on punt returns. He insisted they were more expendable. Each team could carry only twelve Americans on its roster, and the Canadian players usually were not as far advanced, even though some of them were fine athletes.

The switch to the Canadian game was difficult in a number of ways. For one thing, I had to learn to block, something I had never had to do as a single wing tailback. I also had to learn to catch passes, having only thrown them previously. Even though I had played a lot of catch with my brother Joe, who was a fine passer, it was an entirely different game with a great passer like Sam Etcheverry throwing the ball with a lot of zip on it. Under Canadian rules, you can start before the snap of the ball, and I had a hard time adjusting to that. Once I caught on, however, it was my salvation as far as blocking was concerned. It let me hit a lot harder lick when I could build up momentum.

Injuries finally ended my short career with the Alouettes. I don't think I would have been an outstanding pro player any-way. In a sense, I was a man without a position. Single wing tailbacks just didn't have any place in the pro game. I think that in time I could have developed into a receiver or perhaps a de-cent defensive back, but my size would have been a handicap even in those spots. I kept getting hurt, missing games, and slip-ping back on the depth chart. I knew the end was near when Peahead started using me on punt returns.

A Canadian back named Simpson was alternating with me as a kick returner. Simpson was a good player, but he was always doing something to upset Coach Walker, who had one of the sharpest tongues I've ever heard. One day when Peahead was especially exasperated, he shouted, "Simpson, if they put your brain inside a celery seed, it would rattle like hell!"

Another time we were fielding punts while looking into a bright sun. I fumbled a couple of times, and Simpson dropped almost every one. Peahead came charging over and hollered, "What's going on here?"

"We can't see the ball. The sun's in our eyes," Simpson an-swered.

"What the hell do you expect me to do, cause an eclipse?" was Peahead's retort.

I don't know if anyone has ever written a book about Peahead, but somebody should. Undoubtedly there are more stories cir-culating among coaches about Peahead Walker than about Rockne or Neyland or Bryant. He had a low, gravelly voice and a slow, deliberate way of talking in a Southern accent. He was a comical character, even when he was being a disciplinarian, which he was on the football field all the time.

I've never been around a coach who emphasized fundamen-tals more than Peahead did. Everything was blood and guts, with no finesse. He would put us backs through a savage block-ing drill every Tuesday. One day we did so poorly that he made us form a circle and join hands. He called the whole squad in to surround us, and then he had us hold hands and start skipping. He had us skip a few steps to the left and then a few steps to the right.

Finally he turned to the other players and said, "Ain't that the silliest thing you ever saw? A bunch of idiots congratulating themselves on their sorry blocking!"

Peahead is a legend. Bill George, the great linebacker for the Chicago Bears who played his college football under Peahead at Wake Forest, once told about the time he made his recruiting visit. Wake Forest didn't exactly have a scenic campus, and it seems that when Peahead picked him up at the train station in his car, he drove him around the beautiful Duke campus, which was nearby. George, of course, assumed he was seeing Wake Forest. He signed and when he came back that fall to start school, Peahead again met him at the train. This time he drove to Wake Forest.

Bill asked, "What is this place?"

"Why, it's the Wake Forest campus," said Peahead innocently.

"But it's not the same one I saw the last time," said Bill.

"That was the north campus," Peahead responded. "This is the south campus!"

The season was a little over half completed when Coach Walker called me into his office and told me as kindly as he could that I was being cut. He knew that Bowden Wyatt had offered me a job on the Tennessee staff whenever I was free to take it.

Peahead said, "Johnny, you're just not going to be able to stay healthy in pro ball. If I was you, I think I'd just get in coaching right now."

I don't suppose any football player ever exactly enjoyed being cut from the roster, but I left Montreal without any negative feelings at all. I had been treated fairly, I had met a lot of fine people and had made some new friends, and I had enjoyed living in a fascinating place. I loved playing football so much that I would have played until I was forty if I could have done it. That was not going to happen, though, and I had to accept it.

Canadian football begins its season much earlier than the NFL does; so as it turned out, Tennessee was to play its first game in just a few days. I quickly packed my bags and jumped into my black car with the silver streaks on its tail and headed for Knoxville. I arrived in time to see the Vols open the 1957 season against Auburn.

·18·

Low Man on the Totem Pole

I've often thanked my lucky stars for the opportunity to start my coaching career at Tennessee under Bowden Wyatt.

Here I was, doing something I loved to do, on familiar grounds and working at the college level under one of the finest coaches in the game. Not too many young coaches get that kind of break.

As soon as I got back from Canada, I started working. It was too late to put me on the full-time staff, so I had the equivalent of an athletic scholarship, living in the East Stadium dorm and getting my meals and tuition free. Since I still had one quarter of school left before I got my degree, it worked out fine.

At heart I probably was still more a player than a coach. My best buddies were the fellows with whom I had played—Bill Johnson, Tommy Bronson, Frank Kolinsky, Stockton Adkins, Jim Smelcer, and Lon Herzbrun. They were in their senior seasons.

I was the assistant freshman coach in charge of the backs, which remained my basic responsibility throughout the three years I spent on the Vols staff. The head freshman coach was Bobby Proctor, who had played for Wyatt at Arkansas. Bobby and I have been friends ever since, and he has long been recognized as one of the top assistant coaches in college football. He's now on Barry Switzer's staff at Oklahoma.

Bobby and I were more or less in charge of discipline at the dorm, an assignment that traditionally goes to younger staff members. East Stadium was one of the dankest, dreariest places in the world, so we painted it and tried to brighten it up as much as we could.

My old teammate Edd Cantrell and Bob Neyland, Jr., helped out with the freshmen that first year. Bob, who now is an attorney in Kingsport, Tennessee, has long been one of my favorite people. Not long ago he let me have the notebook that his father kept when he was coaching. That's a priceless gift for an old Tennessee football man.

I loved my work on the field. Although I didn't know a thing about being a coach, I could teach technique. Working with the freshman backs was very enjoyable and my first year I was able to coach my brother Bill, who was our number one tailback. I have always thought that in many ways Bill was a better player than I was. One of the best defensive backs I've ever seen, he could do it all on offense—run, pass, and kick. Bob, however, came along at a time when he didn't have a great team supporting him the way I had. However, he had a brilliant freshman year. In his first game he ran a kickoff back about ninety-five yards for a touchdown.

Coach Wyatt put me on full time in January of 1958. I have to admit now that I had no idea of the drive and dedication that it takes to be a successful football coach. I was twenty-two years old, single, making $3,600 a year, and without a care in the world. Even though I always did what I was told to do with enthusiasm, when I didn't have any specific assignment, I usually was over at the student center looking at the girls.

That went on for a few weeks. Then one day when I went to the office, I found a note on my desk. It said, "Congratulations on your work. (Over)"

The flip side said, "When are you going to start?"

Nobody had to tell me who wrote the note. I knew it was from Coach Wyatt.

I swung into action fast! I subscribed to newspapers from all over the east, looking for prospects. I researched the recruiting situation in New England, where we had not enjoyed much success in recent years. If I didn't have any work to do, I invented some. Coach Wyatt got his point across to me without ever having said one word.

Working with my former coaches on the Tennessee staff was a delight. I shared office space with Jim McDonald. I recruited with Skeeter Bailey in Middle Tennessee, with Ralph Chancey in North Carolina and Virginia, and with George Cafego in West Virginia. They all were fine recruiters, and working with them got me started off right. I've heard some coaches say they love everything about college football except the recruiting, but they certainly do not speak for me. I love recruiting. To this day I think it's one of the most challenging and rewarding things that coaches do.

Recruiting with Coach Cafego back in those West Virginia mountains was a rare treat. He had been the tailback coach when I was a player, and he was a real hardnose. He didn't want anyone to think that his tailbacks were pampered; so he sometimes kept us on the practice field thirty minutes longer than the rest of the squad.

Cafego also was rather frugal, as I discovered when I recruited with him. Once when we were driving through snow on back country roads, I was dying for something to drink. I asked him to stop at the next gas station, but he pulled over to the side of the road and stopped.

"Get out and get one of those icicles off that tree and let it melt in your mouth," he ordered.

We were on our way to War, West Virginia, to check on a prospect. For our night's lodging, he stopped at an old hotel that looked as if the next strong wind would blow it to the ground. The floors were covered with lineoleum, and there was one common bathroom for all the guests. I figured Cafego paid about three dollars for the room.

I said, "Come on, Coach. Two-a-days are over. You can let up on me a little now."

He just laughed.

George Cafego is one of the names that always will be associated with Tennessee football. The All-American tailback on the school's first bowl teams back in the late '30s, he later worked with five different Tennessee head coaches, including myself. In his later career, he gained some much-deserved national recognition as a kicking coach. However, his knowledge of the game went a lot deeper than that, and he was one of the fiercest competitors I've ever seen.

Over the years I have come to realize that I owe a debt to Tennessee football that I could never repay. Tennessee gave me a chance to play the game, and then to coach, with one of the great traditions of college football. As I moved along on my career, I found that doors opened more readily for Tennessee men than for some others. For instance, Frank Broyles, later my boss at Arkansas, had an almost reverent respect for Tennessee football. He had played under Bobby Dodd, had gotten his first coaching job under Bob Woodruff, and then had been hired as head coach at Arkansas by John Barnhill. All three were Tennessee men, and all three had played under General Neyland.

The general was the man behind the Tennessee tradition. At one time in the '40s and '50s, he probably had more ex-players holding down major college head coaching jobs than any coach in history—Dodd, Wyatt, Woodruff, Warmath, Herman Hickman, Beattie Feathers, DeWitt Weaver, Phil Dickens, Billy Barnes, Ralph Hatley, Ray Graves, Allyn McKeen, Jim Myers, Clay Stapleton, Bill Meek. That's just some of them. His teaching, particularly on defense and the kicking game, is still followed today.

As a player, I had been in awe of Neyland. I wouldn't have dreamed of starting up a conversation with him. The closest we ever came to a conversation was when we would pass each other and I would say hello. He would grunt. While I was playing, he said some kind things *about* me to the press, comparing me to past Tennessee players I had idolized, but he said almost nothing *to* me. One day shortly after our Sugar Bowl loss to Baylor, I walked into the projection room where the staff was reviewing the game film. I had made a couple of last-man tackles early in the game, and just as I looked in I heard the general say, "If Majors hadn't made those plays, we wouldn't have stayed in the game as long as we did."

Then he looked up and saw me and sort of growled. "If I'd known you were there, I wouldn't have said that," he said.

After I joined the staff, I finally got up enough nerve to talk to him. Instead of being bothered, he seemed to enjoy talking with me. Before long, I was picking his brains while he talked freely about his ideas about football and the principles behind them. I made notes at the time, although I now wish I had kept a diary. I would like to have a record of things like my conversations with Neyland. How many young coaches ever have the chance to get first-hand information from one of the most brilliant minds in football history?

Neyland and Coach Wyatt had great rapport, almost like a father-son relationship. The general came to staff meetings, and sometimes Wyatt and he would disagree about something. Neyland never pushed his opinions too far. After a while he would get up and say, "Well, I've said my piece," and leave.

The day came when it was time for me to leave Tennessee. In 1960 Wade Walker, the head coach at Mississippi State, offered me the job of B team coach at Starkville. The pay was $6,700, a considerable raise over what I was making at Tennessee. Coach Wyatt had just given me a four hundred dollar a year raise after I was married, to $4,000. As I was married, money was more of a factor than it would have been earlier.

But I was happy at Tennessee. I was among old friends and hated the thought of leaving. Jim McDonald gave me some good advice, though. He said, "If you want to grow, go."

I found he was right. If you stay at your old school, there is the danger that you always will be regarded as a former player and never will get the chance to show what you can do. Coach Wyatt asked me to stay; he even took me on a train trip with him to Memphis so we could talk about it. But all along I knew what my decision had to be.

When I was a senior, Coach Wyatt had lent me forty dollars to buy a couple of sport coats. I had never gotten around to repaying him. It would be illegal for a coach to do that today, but it wasn't any kind of inducement. It was just a nice guy helping out a kid who needed it. Before I left for Mississippi State, I walked into his office and plunked down two twenty dollar bills.

"What's that?" he asked.

"That's the forty dollars I've owed you for three years."

"Well, gosh dang it, thank you," he said and put them in his pocket.

So that was the way I said goodbye to Bowden Wyatt, my coach, friend, and mentor. Football lost one of its greatest coaches when he later left the game. Just ask anybody who ever played for him.

·19·

Mary Lynn

I met my future wife in the spring of 1958.

As I hung around the student center, I kept noticing a particularly cute girl, so I asked around until I found out her name was Mary Lynn Barnwell and that she was from Chattanooga. Then I called her dorm and asked her for a date.

She later told me that at first she had me confused with my brother Bill. After that was straightened out, one of her friends told her that John Majors was supposed to be a pretty fast mover, which was more flattering than it was accurate. That almost scared her away from me, but she did give me a date. We hit it off right from the start. It didn't take me long to realize that she was the girl I wanted to marry.

My brother Bill and my sister Shirley Ann both were Tennessee students in the late '50s. At one time Mary Lynn, Shirley Ann, and Bill's girlfriend and future wife, Linnie, lived in the same girls' dorm. I introduced Shirley Ann to Tom Husband, the man she later married. Tom was an end on the football team; so I guess we had to keep it a 100 percent sports family. Shirley Ann was a good athlete herself. She had been a basketball player and a cheerleader at Huntland High.

Mary Lynn and I were married at St. Paul's Episcopal Church in Chattanooga on June 27, 1959. Our first home was a tiny apartment on Cornell near the Armory-Fieldhouse, now called Stokely Center. I didn't command a very princely salary as the junior assistant coach on the staff, and we would have had a hard time making it without friends like Jim and Polly Bradley and "Mister Jim" Thompson.

Jim Bradley, the manager of the Andrew Johnson Hotel and later owner of a restaurant, had been a good friend when I played at Tennessee. Now he often brought Mary Lynn and me steaks to broil; and when we were about to roast in that hot little apartment, he brought us an air conditioner. Mister Jim was the man who ran the Tennessee football training table, one of the best and kindest men I've ever known. We knew we never would go hungry as long as he was around.

We made a southern trip on our honeymoon, stopping first at Atlanta and then at Emmett Lowery's beach motel in Clearwater, Florida. Coach Lowery had been Tennessee's head basketball coach when I was in school. Our last stop was St. Simons Island, Georgia. That's where Jim and Polly Bradley's wedding present caught up with us. It was a big package, beautifully wrapped; and when we opened it, we found a new football and a note: "Just in case you can't find anything else to do on your honeymoon."

Mary Lynn has been everything to me that a wife can be to her husband. She has a great sense of humor, she's smart, and she's obviously beautiful. We share a lot of common interests. We both love to travel and have made several trips overseas together, occasionally with the children. We enjoy all kinds of music, and we love to entertain our friends. She lives her life with as much zest as anybody I know.

We were married before Mary Lynn graduated, but when we came back to Tennessee almost two decades later she went back to school, changed her major, and got a degree in anthropology. She graduated with the winter class of 1984, along with two of my football players, Clyde Duncan and Mike Cofer. Now she is working on her master's degree.

Mary Lynn has a quick mind and an ever-ready quip. We were in Memphis for the Liberty Bowl, riding to a luncheon with her mother and my dad, when I mentioned that I was going to Pittsburgh.

"Pittsburgh? What's in Pittsburgh?" asked Mrs. Barnwell, whereupon Mary Lynn immediately started singing a song that had been popular a few years earlier.

"There's a pawn shop on a corner in Pittsburgh, Pennsylvania. . . ."

Mary Lynn has been a great mother to John Ireland, our son, and to Mary Elizabeth, our daughter. Football coaches have to be away from their kids more than most fathers do, so that puts an even greater burden on their wives. But Mary Lynn has enjoyed every place we've lived—Knoxville, Starkville, Fayetteville, Ames, Pittsburgh, and Knoxville again. She's always adjusted to every culture change, but she says it takes longer each time, which I guess is her way of telling me she wants to stay at Tennessee.

I've been wonderfully blessed in my two families, the one in which I grew up and the one that Mary Lynn and I have shared with our two children. John was born in 1964, and the excitement of Arkansas's winning the national championship that year didn't begin to compare with the joy of having that little guy around the house. I had no idea that babies grew so fast. Recruiting sometimes took me on the road for a full week or more, and when I'd come home I couldn't believe how much he had grown.

Then Mary arrived two years later, one of the prettiest babies I ever saw. I'm just like other fathers about my daughter. She was Daddy's girl, and still is.

Our family almost always has had a dog in the house. Some of them have been "classics." When we were living in Ames, the ugliest-looking little pup you ever saw showed up out of the blue while John was having his sixth birthday party. If there ever has been a Heinz 57-variety dog, that dog was it. His fur was various shades of black, brown, and white; and he had one brown eye and one blue eye. John and Mary adopted him, and he was their daily companion for a couple of years. We named him Pepper.

On one trip from Ames to Sewanee, we let Pepper out of the car for a brief constitutional when we stopped for gas in St. Louis. I suppose there were about a dozen people around the place, and they all kept staring at Pepper. Finally one of them asked, "What kind of dog is that?"

For some unknown reason, at that very instant I remembered a winery near our home in Fayetteville, Arkansas. It was named "Wiedeker Wines," and without thinking about what I was saying I told the man, "He's an Australian Wiedeker."

We had a big laugh about that after we got back into the car, and after that we always told everyone that Pepper was an Australian Wiedeker. I guess he was as close to being that as anything else.

John loves the outdoors, just like his grandfather Majors did. He loves to tramp around in the woods hunting and observing nature, and he loves outdoor sports. He played football at Bearden High in Knoxville, and by a twist of fate he got to play the old single wing system. They put it in for one year, and he was the wingback. As this is being written, he's a junior at Tennessee and a walk-on pole vaulter on the track team. When Mary graduated from high school, she decided to work for a while, and plans to enter college soon.

I love my family. It's hard to express how I feel about them in a book, as I suspect it would be for most people. But as much as I love my job and enjoy travel and golf and being with friends, my greatest pleasure is being at home with Mary Lynn and the kids. And my dogs.

But there'll never be another Australian Wiedeker.

·20·

Happy Days in Starkville

I wouldn't take anything for my experience at Mississippi State. The young coach who stays with one program, even one as good as Tennessee's, really learns only one way of doing things. At Tennessee, and earlier under my dad, I had learned the single wing offense and the wide tackle six defense. At State I was exposed to new concepts on both sides of the ball, the T-formation offense and the Oklahoma "fifty" defense.

Mississippi State always had a hard time getting enough good football players, but it had a unique history of developing top coaches, probably preparing more head coaches for other schools than any other school, going back to the great Bernie Bierman, who built the legendary program at Minnesota in the '30s. Bowden Wyatt coached there as an assistant. Murray Warmath, Darrell Royal, Spook Murphy, Jim Pittman, and several others served as either head coaches or assistants there and then moved on to fame elsewhere. When I was on the staff, first under Wade Walker and then Paul Davis, we had Bill Dooley, Bobby Collins, Frank Jones, Jim Champion, and myself. All of us went on to become head coaches elsewhere.

The atmosphere at Mississippi State was warm and folksy, and I imagine it still is. It is a wonderful environment for young coaches. A number of unforgettable people there have long been associated with the sports program, and they befriended Mary Lynn and me at a time in our lives when we very much needed the reassuring presence of some older friends. Bob Hartley, the longtime sports publicist, is the ultimate Southern gentleman.

Dutch Luchsinger, the tough, leathery old trainer, could scare a young coach half to death.

State didn't always recruit the largest players in the world, and Dutch would hit the ceiling at some of the physical specimens we brought in to be checked. "How many times do I have to tell you not to bring these skinny kids in here?" he'd complain. "Don't you know this is the Southestern Conference?"

Doc Paty, the business manager, always called me "Coachie," and boasted that his buses always ran on time. And then there was Babe McCarthy, who could charm the eyeballs out of a snake and coach a heck of a lot of basketball while he was doing it.

I was the B team coach, which meant that I got to work on both offense and defense. If you approach it with the right attitude, coaching the scout team can be one of the most exciting jobs on a football staff. The B team is composed of kids who are not quite good enough for the varsity, at least not yet, which means they require special attention. Sometimes you have to kick ass with them, but other times you need to love them and hug them because they're sort of like downtrodden children. I was excited about the B team. They were "my" team, and I've never worried or fussed more about any varsity team I've coached than I did about that group.

At the time, students had only three years of eligibility for football; they couldn't play on the varsity as freshmen. Bill Dooley coached the freshmen my first year at Mississippi State, and for both of us the highlight of every week was Thursday afternoon. The varsity would always leave early after a light practice, and then the B team and the freshman team would take over the field.

We would go at each other until dark. We called it the "Toilet Bowl," and we never could find a natural place to stop our games. If we were ahead, Bill would say, "Let's go one more time." If the freshmen were ahead, I'd do the same. Bill and I have been close coaching friends ever since.

We had an excellent staff, especially after my first year when Wade Walker brought in Ken Donahue to coach the defensive line and hired Paul Davis to head up the offense. I have played for and worked with some outstanding coaches in more than thirty years of college football, and I can say with absolute conviction that Donahue and Davis are two of the finest coaches the game has ever had. They love it so much that they could go on coaching until they were eighty and still be working as effectively as they did when they were twenty-five. The football lessons that I learned from them and the help they gave me as I was feeling my way into coaching are things I will never forget.

I don't know that there ever has been a more dedicated football coach than Ken Donahue, with whom I shared a desk for three years at Starkville. We always had great rapport. I knew him from my Tennessee days when he had come there as B team coach while I was a senior, and I had worked with him later when I first joined the staff. Even then he was a master strategist and played to win. One story illustrates that.

My senior year at Tennessee was Donahue's first on the coaching staff. Coach Wyatt always graded the varsity pass defense on how many passes the B team offense could complete in ten tries. The old wide tackle six was a tough defense against deep throws, but it wasn't as strong against shorter passes. When Donahue first took over the B team, Wyatt said, "Okay, let's throw ten and see how we do." The B team completed seven out of ten. Ken knew the weakness of the defense, and he had the B squad throwing nothing but flats and flares. Ralph Chancey, who was the varsity secondary coach, kept yelling, "Let's see some deeps!" but they just kept hitting the little short ones. Ken plays to win.

Paul Davis was the complete football coach. He not only had great knowledge of all phases of the game, he could motivate people to play. Without trying to be a Rockne or Leahy, he could fire up a team better than anybody I ever saw. As an alumnus of Ole Miss, whenever we played them he desperately wanted to win. Ole Miss always had a big advantage in manpower; if we recruited three out of fifty players they wanted, we were doing good. On one trip to Oxford to play Ole Miss, Paul got so worked up during his pregame talk he ran out of superlatives. "I've heard all about these big, fast players they got, but I'll tell you one thing," he said, "we're going out there and play with pride, and we ain't going to take no shit from nobody!"

Henry Lee Parker was another great favorite of mine on the State staff. He was a good-natured fellow from Holly Springs, Mississippi, who coached the offensive and defensive ends. We became good friends with him and his wife, Martha Anne, and years later he joined my staff at Pittsburgh and then came with me to Tennessee as administrative assistant. Martha Ann's brother, "Boo" Ferris, was one of my boyhood heroes. He was an outstanding pitcher for the Boston Red Sox when they played the St. Louis Cardinals in the 1946 World Series, and those two clubs were my favorite big league teams.

We turned the program around at Mississippi State. I say "we" because I was promoted to secondary coach in my second year and became a part of the varsity staff for the first time. State hadn't won a conference game in a long time, but we got a scoreless tie with Tennessee at Memphis in 1960. That was a proud moment for me. My first big assignment was to scout the Vols, and I didn't leave out anything. I told them more about Tennessee than they really needed to know. After I had been talking for a full hour, while demonstrating all the stances and fakes and drop steps, everybody was starting to squirm. Finally Henry Lee said, "Johnny, we really didn't want a book on the single wing!"

By 1961 we were a competitive team, and we beat an outstanding Auburn team at Birmingham, 11-10, in a big win. Johnny Baker caught a pass for a two-point conversion to give us the victory. Baker was one of those players who underwent a personality change on the field. In real life he was a very religious, soft-spoken, gentle person. But once the whistle blew on Saturday afternoon, he would kill you. In the loss to Tennessee at Knoxville earlier that season, Johnny put two Vol tailbacks— Glenn Glass and Mallon Faircloth—out of commission on consecutive plays.

Little Bobby Morton, who probably didn't weigh 155 pounds, was Tennessee's third string tailback that day. Later Coach Wyatt told me that when Baker dropped Faircloth, he turned to the bench and yelled, "Morton!"

Nobody said anything for a while, and finally Bobby responded in a very small voice, "Who, me, Coach?"

After the game Coach Walker reprimanded Baker about the rough stuff. Johnny, who was a very sensitive boy, went home to Meridian, Mississippi, and Henry Lee had to go to his home to talk him into coming back. Later, Johnny was a good professional football player and today is a successful businessman.

Late in the 1962 season Coach Walker dropped a bombshell on us at a Sunday staff meeting. He told us he wasn't going to coach the next year. "I hope to stay on as athletic director, and I'm going to recommend that Paul Davis become the head coach," he said.

Dave "Dog" Owens, a colorful Mississippi sports figure, had just joined our staff that September after a great high school coaching career at Meridian. As we walked out of the conference room with everybody wondering what the future held, Dog broke the tension. "I guess I just had the shortest tenure in college football history," he said.

Paul Davis was named head coach and took Mississippi State to its first bowl game in twenty years in 1963. We went 6-2-2 and easily could have been unbeaten. We lost to Alabama and Joe Namath, 20–19, and to a good Memphis State team. The ties were with Florida and Ole Miss, and the Rebels had to kick a field goal in the final minute to get the tie and win the Southeastern Conference championship.

Mississippi State wasn't a big drawing card, and the best bid we could get was to the Liberty Bowl at Philadelphia. About 7,000 people turned out in 100,000-seat Kennedy Stadium to see us beat North Carolina State on one of the coldest football days I've ever experienced. But it was a bowl game, and we were happy.

People from Mississippi State receive a lot of teasing because of the school's rural setting, and there is little danger of getting caught up in the social whirl in Starkville. But Mary Lynn and I enjoyed its pace as much as any place we have lived. For the first two years we rented a very nice apartment in the university housing complex near the stadium for 23 dollars a month, including utilities. After that, at Mary Lynn's insistence, we moved to a house on Bulldog Boulevard for 67 dollars a month. I accused her of social climbing.

In Starkville people invented their own entertainment. I love to dance, and when a little dance club was formed Mary Lynn and I were regular attenders, along with most of the other coaches and their wives. We learned all the new steps, including the cha cha, which became the specialty of Mary Earle Davis,

Paul's wife, and me. Every time Mary Earle and I talk, she wants to know when we're going to do the cha cha again.

During my four years at State, I met a lot of people in coaching who later became good friends. One was Gil Brandt of the Dallas Cowboys, who even then had the reputation for being one of pro football's greatest scouts. Gil soon had me doing scouting reports on our players and on leading Southeastern Conference players. The highest mark I ever gave was to Leroy Jordan, the Alabama linebacker whom the Cowboys drafted.

One night I was awakened by a phone call from Gil. He was driving Leroy Jordan's new Toronado, which was one of his bonuses for signing with the Cowboys, through Starkville on Highway 82 when he hit a cow.

"I can't understand your state laws," he said. "This farmer's cow tore up the car, and he tells me he's going to sue me to pay for his cow. I threatened to sue him, and he just laughed. He said he was the sheriff's brother!"

During those years, Darrell Royal of Texas and Frank Broyles of Arkansas were the hottest articles in college coaching. I was happy at Mississippi State, but I told Mary Lynn that if I ever had a chance to work for either one of them, it would be hard to turn down the opportunity. Somebody must have been reading my mind, because shortly after the 1963 season ended, Paul Davis called me into his office and told me that Frank Broyles had requested permission to talk to me about a job on his staff.

·21·

Lessons from Professor Broyles

Frank Broyles sent a plane from Fayetteville for Mary Lynn and me. When we arrived, we discovered he had arranged a social gathering and had invited all the coaches and their wives to meet us. Including the wives was one of those extra touches so typical of Broyles. Football coaches spend so much time away from home that it is very important for their wives to know each other well and to be able to lean on one another at times. Frank was way ahead of most head coaches in thinking of what would help his coaches and players, on the field and off, as professionals and as people.

Coach Broyles offered me the job of coaching the defensive secondary, and after I talked with him I knew I would take it. But I dreaded having to break the news to Paul Davis. He and I were so close, and Mary Lynn and Mary Earle were such good friends, that I put off telling him for as long as I could. Since then I've always been able to empathize with the football prospect who hates to tell a coach that he is going to sign with another school. For that reason I've long favored moving forward the date for signing the national letter of intent to enable the students to get the agony over with a little sooner. It's been moved up some, but I would like for it to be even earlier.

When I told Frank I would like to have the job, he said the pay would be $11,000 a year. I was making $7,500 at Mississippi State. Then I did a pretty silly thing. I didn't want Frank to think that I was making the move just for the money; I have never done that in any job I have taken. I said, "You don't have to pay me that much."

Fortunately, Frank was smooth enough that he was able to handle it without causing any more embarrassment for me than I had already brought on myself. He told me that the salary was included in the budget for whoever was hired.

Frank Broyles is one of the smartest men I've ever known in football. He not only has a great knowledge of the game himself, on both offense and defense, but he is a master of taking other people's ideas and improving them for his program. When I joined the Arkansas staff, he already was getting into the I formation, which was new to the Southwest Conference. He brought in John McKay from Southern California to explain the fine points of the I to the coaching staff. On defense, he was using the monster alignment that took the strong side advantage away from the opponents' offense.

Frank also developed a system of rotating his assistant coaches that worked to their benefit. In his early years, Hayden Fry was the offensive backfield coach and Doug Dickey handled the defensive secondary. When Hayden got the head coaching job at Southern Methodist, Dickey moved over to the offense and Bill Pace came from Kansas to take over the secondary. When Doug left to become Tennessee's head coach in 1964, Bill moved from defense to offense and I was hired to replace him. Three years later, Bill got the head coaching job at Vanderbilt, and I switched to offense and Hootie Ingram came in as secondary coach. The offensive backfield coach called plays from the coach's booth in the press box. That experience was invaluable for an assistant who wanted to be a head coach someday.

Frank's innovations covered a lot of territory. Arkansas may have been the only school in the country where the assistant coaches were voted a housing supplement by the state legislature; we received a check every month. Somehow he lined up a television show for his assistant coaches. I was on it my last two years at Arkansas, and every Thursday night we would fly to Little Rock to do the show.

In addition, Frank also started a program that enabled his assistants to get complimentary cars from automobile dealers in the area. Along with Bob Devaney of Nebraska, Frank probably did more than any other college football coach to raise the level of pay for assistant coaches throughout the profession. When I left Arkansas, I was making $18,000, almost as much as I was offered for the head coaching job at Iowa State.

Frank could also be a snake oil salesman when the situation required it. We had great teams for the first three years I was there, 1964 through 1966, but in 1967 we had to start all over with a very green team and ended up losing seven games. However, you never could tell we were a losing team from Frank's Sunday TV show. He'd re-run the good plays, talk about how this player or that player was coming along, and before the program was over everybody would be feeling good about the team. One night I arrived at home from the office just as Mary Lynn finished watching Frank's show.

"You know," she said, "until I saw Frank on TV, I would have sworn we lost that game yesterday."

Although he let his assistants do most of the coaching, Frank always was ready to challenge us. We had to be prepared when we went to staff meetings, because we never knew when we might have to go to the blackboard and diagram something. And we had better be right.

Frank was a mover and a shaker, a man of great imagination. Nevertheless, in spite of all his innovations and new ways of doing things, he always reverted to his background in times of stress. He was a pupil of Bobby Dodd, who had been a pupil of General Neyland, and when things got tough on the field he would take us back to the fundamentals—field position, kicking game, defense.

He could get mad, too. In those years Texas Tech had a great running back, Donny Anderson, and Arkansas was never able to do much about him. In 1963, the year before I joined the staff, the two teams had played a great offensive battle, up and down the field, first one team and then the other taking the lead. Finally, Arkansas went on top with just a few minutes left to play. Tech took the kickoff and started moving. Anderson would make ten yards here, then twelve there. Frank stomped up and down the sidelines, his red hair waving in the breeze. Jim McKenzie was calling the defensive plays in the press box. Finally Frank turned to Wilson Matthews, who was on the sideline phone.

"You tell McKenzie I want him (Anderson) stopped, and I want him stopped right now!" he yelled.

Frank didn't say how to do it. He just said to do it. And somehow the defense finally stopped Anderson, and Arkansas won the game.

What a great adventure my first year at Arkansas was! We won all ten regular season games and then beat Nebraska in the Cotton Bowl to win the national championship. It's the only perfect year, including the regular season and the bowl game, that the Razorbacks ever have had. The team had been 5–5 the previous year and, although we knew we had good material in '64, we still didn't have great overall talent. In the spring Coach Broyles showed the players and the staff the movies of the Rose, Cotton, Sugar, and Orange Bowl games and said, "Here's what the winners are doing. We're going to work our butts off to see if we can't do the same thing."

Working with the defensive secondary was a great pleasure. My best player was Kenny Hatfield, who later joined Doug Dickey's staff at Tennessee and now is back at Arkansas as a very successful head coach. Kenny was a great safety, leading the nation in kick returns that year. In our biggest win—with Texas, of course—Kenny ran a punt back eighty yards in the fourth quarter to put us ahead, 14–7. Texas then drove back down the field and scored a touchdown in the last minute or two of play, but Billy Gray knocked down a pass in the end zone as they tried for a two-point conversion. We won, 14–13. Billy is now Kenny's recruiting coordinator at Arkansas.

Darrell Royal showed real class after that game. We knew that losing by one point had to have been terrible for him—Texas was the defending national champion and was ranked number one at the time—but he came to the Arkansas dressing room and made a talk to our team that I'll always remember. He said, "Since we had to lose, we don't want to lose to anybody less than the national champions. We want you guys to go on and win 'em all." That was not an empty gesture; he meant it.

A lot of people assume coaches learn only from head coaches in this business, but that's wrong. Through the years I've learned as much from assistants as I have from the head coaches, and at Arkansas we had some really great football minds on the staff. I learned from Bill Pace every chance I got. Bill had a very calculating mind, like a good bridge player; and he always stayed cool in emergency situations. He and his wife,

Joan, became as close friends as Mary Lynn and I ever had. Some years later I was very fortunate to be able to bring him to Tennessee as our offensive coordinator. He did a great job for us in 1981, when we went from a terrible start to an 8–4 record and a bowl victory.

Everybody on the Arkansas staff was aware of Jim McKenzie's great abilities, and every time a good head coaching job came open we always pulled for him to get it. When that finally happened, what seemed to be a very happy story had a tragic ending. Jim got the head coaching job at Oklahoma in 1966, coached one year, and then died suddenly of a heart attack. All of us learned so much from Jim, and I was heartbroken to hear of his death.

Other great football minds at Arkansas included Wilson Matthews, who coached the linebackers, and Merv Johnson, the offensive line coach. Barry Switzer came along later as the receiver coach. Today Merv is Barry's assistant head coach at Oklahoma. And Jimmy Johnson, who was the Arkansas nose guard in my first season there, later joined the staff as a graduate assistant. Jim later worked on my staff at Iowa State and today is head coach at Miami of Florida.

I was the secondary coach again in 1965, when we were 10–0 and made another appearance in the Cotton Bowl. I had the same position in 1966, when we were 8–2 and went nowhere. We started the last game needing a win over Texas Tech at Lubbock to nail down our third straight conference championship, and that game taught me something about the dangers of complacency.

We had gone to two straight Cotton Bowls, and some of the people got to talking about how nice it would be to go somewhere else for a change, to Miami or New Orleans. I guess we got what we deserved. Tech stopped us three times at the one-yard line, and we lost the game. We still could have gone to the Cotton Bowl if Texas Christian had beaten Southern Methodist that day; so we held up the team bus after the game to listen to its finish on the radio. With less than two minutes left, TCU was leading by a couple of points. All they had to do was to punt the ball, but SMU blocked it and scored. And so went the Cotton Bowl.

Frank was furious. We got some other bowl offers, but he just said, "No bowls." And that was that.

In 1967 I was given the opportunity to coach the offensive backs and to call the plays, a great break for me. I hadn't worked with the offense since I had coached the B team at Mississippi State six years earlier. I had kept up with offensive strategy; you have to do that as a defensive coach. But I badly needed the practice field and game experience on offense.

Frank was very helpful to me. He was an expert T-quarterback coach himself, and his thinking on offense helped me have an offensive plan ready to take with me when I went to Iowa State the next year.

Those were happy years for Mary Lynn and me. We rented a house from John Barnhill, the athletic director and one of the wisest men I've ever known, for the first three years. It was right across from the football stadium, and we were close to the other young coaching couples, like Bill and Joan Pace, Barry and Kay Switzer, Jim and Sue McKenzie, and Merv and Cindy Johnson. Both of our children were born while we were there, John Ireland in 1964 and Mary Elizabeth in 1966.

The only cloud in my memories of Arkansas had nothing to do with Arkansas itself. We were living there when an awful tragedy struck the Majors family.

✦22✦

My Brother Bill

Saturday, October 16, 1965, was one of the most exciting days I ever had experienced in football. Our Arkansas team drove eighty yards in the last four minutes to pull from behind and beat Texas, 24–21. When I read the newspaper the next morning, I found that my old Tennessee team, where my brother Bill was the defensive secondary coach, had played Alabama to a 7–7 tie when Kenny Stabler lost track of the situation and threw the ball out of bounds on fourth down. It had been a while since the Vols had given Alabama a good game. Mary Lynn and I had houseguests from Tennessee that weekend, Kleber Duncan and his wife; and we spent some happy hours talking about those two games. "Dunk" is a Tennessee alumnus who has been a good friend of Bowden Wyatt and Skeeter Bailey.

On Monday morning I received a telephone call from George Cafego in Knoxville. He said, "Johnny, I've got some bad news for you. Little Billy is dead."

At first I didn't understand. I had the notion that he was talking about one of Bill's little boys, Bo or Mark. But then George told me that my brother Bill and two other fine young coaches, Charlie Rash and Bobby Jones, had been killed in a car-train accident on their way into the office early that morning.

My feelings were indescribable. To this day I cannot talk about them. Bill's death was the most devastating thing that has ever happened to me, but even then I knew my pain was nothing compared to what my mother and father and Bill's wife, Linnie, were feeling. I had my wife and son, and I had a challenging job to keep me occupied. They had lost a son and a husband.

Frank Broyles made arrangements for a pilot to fly me to Sewanee, where my parents lived, on a private plane. I've never taken a trip that seemed longer, even though it probably took less than two hours. I just could not come to terms with what had happened.

By the time I arrived at home, Mother and Daddy had already left for Knoxville. The rest of the family assembled at Sewanee and drove over in a couple of cars. A beautiful memorial service was held at the Church Street Methodist Church for Bill and the other two coaches. The next day we went back to Lynchburg for the funeral services. Being there among old friends who had been so much a part of our lives helped tremendously.

In a way, Bill was the one who was closest to all of us. Coming along in the middle of the family, he played a lot with Joe and me, who were older; he also played with Shirley Ann and Larry, who came after him. And he was a big buddy to little brother Bob, helping him learn to pass and kick. Bob came to Tennessee to see Bill play as often as Daddy would let him.

I never had seen Daddy floored by anything, but for several years after Bill's death he was almost a different person. He went on with his coaching, of course, and in time he became pretty much his old self again. But to the day he died, something that had always been there was missing.

Mother later told me that she knew something terrible had happened when Daddy answered the telephone that morning, even before he told her the news. "I knew it when he walked down the stairs," she said. "His step had always been so quick, so brisk. I had never seen him walk like that before."

Each of the Majors family has special memories of Bill. When we were kids and Bill would get tired of my bossing him around, Daddy would say, "Pick up something and throw it at him." That's when we learned that Bill had a strong arm. He was only three or four years old at the time, but he'd grab a rock or a mudball—anything—and let it fly. He put some good knots on me before I learned to get out of range in a hurry.

The Majors family always has been close and loving. However, if someone who doesn't know us should drop in on a family gathering, he'd swear that we were mortal enemies. We fuss and argue constantly, over any subject that comes up, whether we know anything about it or not. Bill was in his element in those situations. He had a sharp, analytical mind, and none of the rest of us was ever able to beat him in cards.

The last good visit I had with Bill was when Mary Lynn and I spent the night with Linnie and Bill in Knoxville. He and I stayed up half the night arguing over everything under the sun. We'd get so worked up that if one of us had to go to the bathroom, the other would follow him in there to keep the conversation going. Mary Lynn and Linnie couldn't understand that, but we were that excited and happy at being together again.

Bill eventually would have been a head coach, I'm sure. And he would have been a great one. At the age of twenty-five, he already had reached a high level of responsibility as secondary coach. He had a great knowledge of the game and a way of relating to his players. He was as honest as any man I've ever known, and I don't know of anyone who ever knew him who didn't like him. Later, brother Bob came to Tennessee and wore Bill's old number, 44, with great pride. Even now, when I look out on the field and see number 44 on one of our Tennessee players, I think of Bill. Incidentally, Bill's oldest son, Bo, wore number 44 as a linebacker at Austin Peay State University.

Bill's sons, Bo and Mark, are grown men now. When we all go back to visit Mother at Christmas, they take their daddy's place in our family pickup basketball games. We go down to the Sewanee gym and play by our own set of rules, which basically means no rules at all—pushing and shoving and scratching, forever competing the way Bill always did. Those Sewanee visits, with the basketball games, poker games, and family bull sessions, were among the best times I've ever had in my life.

Bill was the first of the family to leave us. I don't think any of us ever had stopped to think that some day, sooner or later, there would be an empty place that never could be filled again.

But there was. And there is. And there always will be.

·23·

The Challenge at Ames

Iowa State University had long been known as a graveyard for football coaches, so a lot of people were surprised when I accepted the head coaching job there in late November of 1968. None of them were more surprised than Johnny Majors.

I had no earthly intention of taking the job when I went to Ames for my first interview and had begun to look around for potential head coaching jobs. I had been interviewed by Vanderbilt a year earlier, before my good friend, Bill Pace, was picked for the position. Also, I had been interested in the North Carolina job that year, although I hadn't applied for it. Another old buddy, Bill Dooley, got that one. I never have liked the idea of going against good friends for a coaching job, and I have actually kept my name out of a number of situations to avoid it.

Iowa State certainly wasn't on my list. The Cyclones had to compete in the toughest conference in the nation, the Big Eight, with a very small stadium and a football budget to match. In the years before I arrived, the team had been winning only a couple of games a year.

When I had talked to Coach Barnhill about moving on to a head job, he had said that the first thing to do in becoming a head coach was to make sure I had a chance to win. "You need to get your feet wet sooner or later," he said. "But you don't want to get in up to your ass in mud!"

Consequently, when Clay Stapleton, the Iowa State athletic director, called to ask me to come for an interview, I told him I wasn't interested. "I'd just be wasting your time and money," I said.

"Well, come on up and visit with us, anyway," he answered. "What have you got to lose?"

I had an idea of what he had in mind. He needed to bring in some coaches who would tell the school administration what Iowa State had to do to upgrade the football program, even if they were not interested in the job. Clay was an old Tennessee man who had played under General Neyland and John Barnhill, and he had been a fine coach himself. His famous "Dirty Thirty" team of the previous decade had been one of the few good Iowa State teams since World War II. I figured one ex-Vol ought to be courteous to another one, so I agreed to an interview.

Clay brought in a number of men who eventually became head coaches: Al Onofrio, who later succeeded Dan Devine at Missouri; Rudy Feldman, later the head coach at New Mexico; Carl Selmer, later the head man at Miami of Florida; and Erk Russell, Vince Dooley's long-time assistant at Georgia, who became the head coach of Georgia Southern's NCAA Division II national champions. I don't know for sure, but I expect that most of them visited more to help Clay impress the administration with the needs of the football program than to go after the job.

I flew to Des Moines from Dallas, where I was on a recruiting trip. When I stepped out of the plane at the Des Moines airport, I was met by Bob Dillon, the president of KRNT radio and television. His stations handled the Iowa State broadcasts, and he was to become one of the most influential people in my life.

Bob was decked out in a tuxedo. "This is the way we meet all our coaching candidates," he laughed. Actually, he had a formal dinner engagement later in the day.

No one individual was more responsible for Iowa State's resurgence in college football than Bob Dillon was. As a member of the athletics council, he supported me in every possible way, and he became my closest friend and advisor. I never would have taken the job if it had not been for him; and although I live far from Ames, we have maintained the same kind of close relationship we enjoyed there. Next to my father, he has been the most influential male figure in my life.

I was honest with the committee. I told them during the interview that I had no intention of taking the job. I had prepared for the occasion because I figured the experience would help me in future interviews. I must have done pretty well because after it was over they called me back in and offered me the job!

I told them I would need some time to think about it. Bob Dillon drove me back to Des Moines to catch a plane back to Dallas, and during that ride he said some things that made me look at the Iowa State situation in a different light.

He quoted from Shakespeare: "There is a tide in the affairs of men which taken at the flood leads on to fortune." Then he said, "You're on the twenty-yard line of your life, and if I were you I'd go for the long gainer."

Back in Dallas, I called Daddy and brought him up to date on the situation. He listened until I was finished. Then he said, "You know that I am not going to tell you whether to take that job or not, but I will tell you one thing. There are a lot of great football coaches in the Big Eight, but if you decide to take that job I don't want you ever to look across the field in awe of anybody. Lay your ears back and go to work!"

A few days later, December 8, 1967, I went back to Ames for a second visit, still fully intending to say no, and said yes. I was a head coach at thirty-two.

What a small world this is. When I met with the Iowa State president, Dr. W. Robert Parks, that day, he noticed on my resumé that I came from Lynchburg, Tennessee. "Did you ever know a Shirley Majors from down there?" he asked.

"I ought to know him. He's my father," I answered.

"I played high school basketball against him," he said. "I'm from Mulberry, myself."

Mulberry is a little place about halfway between Lynchburg and Fayetteville. It has no high school, and Dr. Parks had gone to Fayetteville High.

When Dr. Parks said the job carried a $20,000 salary, I did the same thing I did when interviewing with Frank Broyles, only in reverse. "I'll need twenty-one thousand," I said.

I have no idea why I said that. The money didn't matter that much to me. I guess I just wanted to demonstrate that I could drive a hard bargain.

Dr. Parks pulled a little book out of his desk drawer, turned to a certain page, and then said, "That won't be any problem." Clay Stapleton told me later that he had consulted the Iowa public records to make sure that I wouldn't be making more than Ray Nagel, the coach at the University of Iowa.

I hadn't expected to take the job, so I had no extra clothes with me, not even a change of underwear. Nevertheless, I went right to work that day. A reception was being held at the Gibbs-Cook heavy equipment company in Des Moines, and I rode there with Clay and Edith Stapleton. As we drove along, Clay said, "See what a beautiful state Iowa is."

I looked around the countryside. It was cold, dreary, and overcast. I couldn't see a sign of a hill in any direction and I thought, *How in the world can I ever recruit football players to come here?* Later on I grew to appreciate what Bob Dillon calls the "verdant soil" of Iowa. It isn't flat. It is gently rolling; and when the grass is green and the corn is high, Iowa is a beautiful state.

The next day, equipped with new underwear and socks, I set out with Ray Donnells of the Cyclone Club booster group, on my first fund-raising trip. We drove to Creston, a town in the southwestern part of the state. One of the club's activities was a "Pork and Beef in the Line Club" that enabled people to donate pigs and calves for the training table. We stopped in a little town on the way, and Ray dropped in on a banker-farmer he knew to ask him for a contribution. The man said he'd be glad to donate a calf for the cause. A couple of months later we made the same trip and stopped by to see our benefactor.

"I'm awfully sorry, Ray, but your calf died," he said. He probably had several hundred calves, and ours had to be the one that died!

I never have been as discouraged as I was during those first few weeks at Ames. Mary Lynn and the kids still were in Fayetteville, and I was living in a motel room. The weather was unbelievably cold, and I was having a terrible time trying to put a staff together. Most of the coaches I knew were from the South and didn't want to come that far north. At the time I couldn't blame them.

I had inherited a 2–9 football team with inadequate facilities, a dinky little stadium, and no tradition. I was on the go all day every day, recruiting and making talks, and at night I would walk the floor. I experienced the same anxiety I had undergone the summer before I left Huntland for Tennessee. I took my pulse frequently during that time, and my heartbeat was about thirty beats a minute over my norm.

However, what appeared to be disadvantages in hiring a staff turned out to be a plus in the long run. Since we couldn't pay top money for experienced assistants, I hired some young, energetic, outgoing coaches who didn't mind the long hours and weren't intimidated by the talk about a football graveyard. I brought in Gordon Smith from the Arkansas staff to be receiver coach. Jackie Sherrill, a student assistant at Arkansas who had played for Bear Bryant at Alabama, came to coach the B team. Jimmy Johnson, our former nose guard at Arkansas, had just become unemployed when the Wichita State staff was fired, and he joined us as defensive line coach. Swede Lee, a former high school coach from Texarkana, Arkansas, was the defensive coordinator. I kept one member of the old Iowa State staff, Lou Erber, as offensive backfield coach; and I hired one high school coach, Jack Blazek, from Marshalltown, Iowa.

Joe Madden, an old friend who had been a graduate assistant at Mississippi State when I was there, was a member of the Wake Forest staff by this time. Joe kept recommending people to me. At the coaches convention in New York, he said, "John, if you still need a secondary coach, why not hire me?"

"Why in the dickens didn't you tell me you were available before this?" I laughed. So Joe joined my staff and stayed with me for eleven years at Iowa State, Pittsburgh, and Tennessee. I don't know what I would have done without him. He was a bundle of energy, always involved in every part of the operation. His wife, Jan, and Mary Lynn became the best of friends, and our kids— their four and our two—grew up together in three different cities. Joe now coaches in pro football with the Atlanta Falcons, but the Maddens and the Majors always will be close.

Swede Lee was a bit older than the rest of us, and he had left coaching for the insurance business for a year before he joined us. All the Southerners on the staff were a bit depressed by the strange surroundings and the cold weather, Swede most of all. He never did quite adjust. At one Sunday afternoon staff meeting in midwinter, I divided the state of Iowa into four recruiting areas. I gave Gordon Smith the northeast corner, Jimmy Johnson the southeast, and took the Des Moines area for myself.

"Swede, you can take the southwest," I said.

"Johnny, you'd better split it up three ways, because I'm going back to Arkansas," he replied.

I don't remember this specifically, but Jimmy Johnson says I just handed him the keys to my car and, without looking up, said, "Jimmy, take Swede back to the airport."

That left us without a defensive coordinator. At Jimmy's suggestion, I hired Larry Lacewell, who had been with him at Wichita State. Larry was a smart guy with an Alabama and Arkansas background. He was the kind of young, confident sort of coach who blended in with the rest of the staff.

Looking back, I think that those months were the most exciting time of my life. That young staff worked together and played together with tremendous zest. It was the most competitive group of people I've ever been around. We would compete in a game of charades at a party as if it were a football game. Once we made a date to go ice skating, a brand new adventure for all us southern boys. Jimmy Johnson sneaked out and took lessons. When the big day came the rest of us fell all over the ice, but Jimmy went gliding along like Hans Brinker on his silver skates. You have to get up early to keep up with Jimmy Johnson.

Look at what those coaches have done since then. Sherrill has been head coach at Washington State, Pittsburgh, and Texas A & M; Johnson at Oklahoma State and Miami; and Lacewell at Arkansas State. Joe Madden was assistant head coach at both Pittsburgh and Tennessee before moving to the pros. And three others who joined us later, Joe Avezzano, Ray Green, and Ollie Keller, all became head coaches. George Haffner, another later addition, is now Vince Dooley's offensive coordinator at Georgia.

The wives were even more popular than their husbands. I don't guess there's ever been a prettier bunch of coaches' wives on one staff than the crew we had at Iowa State!

Those young coaches ranged all over the state of Iowa, and they became immensely popular with alumni, football fans, and high school coaches. They were all good recruiters, and when Avezzano and Ray Green—our first black coach—joined us the second year, we had two new supersalesmen on the staff.

One prospect told a sportswriter that "that guy at Iowa State reminds me of *The Music Man!*" And he was right, in a way. We were trying to put a band together, and we still didn't have any instruments.

I set out to make Iowa State football an "in" thing on campus. I visited every fraternity and sorority house and every dorm. I made a speech to the students on apathy, and nothing could have been more appropriate. Only about seventy-five of them turned up in the huge assembly hall. But I gave them the whole dose, just as if there had been a packed house.

Like many schools of the late 60s, Iowa State had its share of student unrest. During my first summer, there was a black boycott at the school. Out of 20,000 students, only 200 were black. I think the protestors said some important things; there were some wrongs that needed to be corrected. Some of our players asked me to hire a black coach.

"I agree with you," I said, "but I don't know any black coaches. I'll look for one as quickly as possible, but he'll have to be good. I won't hire anybody just because he's black."

Well, I found Ray Green the next year, and he became a vital member of our staff.

However, the immediate problem was that six black players wanted to bring grievances against me. They said they would not talk to me unless they could bring an outside representative with them. I always had an open door policy with my players, -but I refused to meet with them on those terms. I would have responded the same way to any group, but one of our best tackles, Willie Muldrew, decided not to return to Iowa State that fall. Willie was shot to death that summer by his girl friend in an incident unrelated to football. But it was a tragedy that weighed heavily on me, and on the team.

I did not face an easy situation at Iowa State, but I had the backing of Clay Stapleton, Dr. Parks, and the athletics council. They agreed to let us go $100,000 beyond the budget that first year, something I have always thought showed great foresight on their part. As my wise friend Bob Dillon said during the discussion, "Budgets are made to be broken, if they are broken intelligently."

In five years' time a red-ink program was solidly in the black, and the stadium was in the process of being enlarged to a capacity of 40,000. Those things would not have happened if the school's administration had not been able to look beyond the present to get a glimpse of tomorrow.

·24·

The Band Kept Playing

We didn't have a very good football team at Iowa State in 1968, so I decided that at least we would be entertaining

I pulled out every cow pasture play I knew. We used double reverses and the Statue of Liberty and quick huddle plays. Also, going against my conservative Tennessee background, I called fake punts five or six times on fourth down in our own territory.

Clay Stapleton just shook his head at that. He was a Neyland man through and through, and during his time as the coach of Iowa State he had been roundly criticized for his conservatism. Two of the team's most avid supporters were Bob and Lucretia Sprowell, who lived in Ames. Lucretia had given Clay a hard time for kicking on third down, so after I had unleashed some of my tricks, Clay wrote her a letter.

"Dear Lucretia," it said. "I hope you're satisfied. You gave me hell for kicking on third down. Now we've got a coach who won't even kick on fourth down!"

We won our very first game that season, beating Buffalo University, 28–10, at Ames. Even though Buffalo was not a great team, it still was a historic day for me. Every coach's biggest victory is the first one. We showed some discipline and organization on the field and we didn't do silly things like jumping offsides. We made a good first impression on the fans.

However, we won only one Big Eight game in 1968, against Vince Gibson's Kansas State team, winding up 3–7 for the year. Since that was an improvement from the previous season, we were optimistic for the future.

Unfortunately, we only went 3–7 in 1969, too, a record that didn't look nearly as good the second year. We were no match for teams like Oklahoma, Nebraska, Colorado, and Missouri. When Oklahoma State beat us in the last game of the year, I was as down in the dumps as I ever have been as a coach. I couldn't figure out in what direction we were headed.

The next day I called a staff meeting and told the coaches to put on their traveling shoes. "You're going to hit the road and stay out there until we get the kind of football players we need to play in this league," I said. "Call me when you need me to help, and I'll be there."

We had a $25,000 recruiting budget, and I decided to bust it. I think I am as much a stickler for following the rules as anybody, but I knew that we could never compete in the Big Eight if we didn't get Big Eight talent. And we had to have it right now if we expected to keep our jobs.

Two or three weeks later, Bob Fellinger, the athletics chairman, and Clay Stapleton, called me in for a conference. "Johnny, you've overspent the recruiting budget," Bob said.

"Okay, I'll see what I can do," I answered.

I left the athletic director's office for mine, about a block away, to call the guys in off the road. I never got past the steps. Instead, I turned and walked back into Clay's office and said, "We're going down the drain if we don't get the players we need. I'm not going to bring the coaches back. You can fire me or do what you want, but we don't have a chance if we call 'em back."

Clay Stapleton and Bob Fellinger and the council backed me. We went $15,000 over the budget, and it was the smartest money Iowa State ever spent on football. Our coaches brought in the best class of signees in the school's history: Ike Harris, a wide-out who could run a 4.6 forty; Mike Strachan, a great running back who later became a long-time pro; Keith Krepfle, one of the best tight ends I've ever seen, also a pro star later; Lawrence "Big Daddy" Hunt, a huge, strong defensive tackle from Lawrence, Kansas; and a number of other fine athletes.

I figure that $15,000 saved my career. It certainly saved Iowa State football. Our program would not have survived without it, and not too many schools are interested in coaches with poor track records. As Bob Dillon said when the council was discussing it, "Sometimes it pays to break the budget, if you do it wisely."

Everybody was excited when our 1970 team won its first three games against nonconference opposition. I was guilty of letting myself get carried away, and before our first Big Eight game at Colorado I told the coaches, "We're ready." Famous last words!

Cliff Branch returned three punts for touchdowns against us in the first quarter, and we wound up getting beaten, 61–10, the most points ever scored against a team I coached. Once again I found myself wondering where I was heading professionally. I had thought that we would have a decent team, and now we seemed to be back on the same old treadmill.

However, two great victories saved the season for us. We beat a good Kansas team, 24–10, at Lawrence, Kansas. And then we beat Missouri, 31–19, at Columbia. It was the first time in thirty-two years that the Cyclones had beaten the Tigers on their home field, and they had beaten us badly in our two previous meetings.

Most people expected more of the same in this game. But we had a great sophomore quarterback named George Amundson who really came into his own that day. Amundson was the best athlete I've ever coached. While Tony Dorsett was the best football player, Amundson was the total athlete. He was about six feet, three inches, tall and weighed 212 pounds; he could run strong and throw well, and he had supreme confidence. He played tailback in his junior year, to fill a big hole we had there, and he was a great track athlete. For a long time he held Big Eight records in the shot and discus.

I put in an option series for the Missouri game. Since we had two good quarterbacks, Amundson and Dean Carlson, I figured the option series was a good way to exploit their strengths. The game wasn't very old before Carlson had gone twenty yards on the option for a touchdown, and later Amundson made option runs of thirty-five and seventy-one yards for scores.

We led, 31–19, with just a few minutes left and all we had to do was hold onto the ball, so I told George to run sneaks. George had a little of the hot dog in him. Sometimes on sprintout passes in practice, he would throw the ball between his legs. It usually hit the target, but it drove me up the wall. Most quarterbacks tuck the ball away on sneaks, but George held the ball straight out in front of him with his arms extended and leaped just as high and far as he could. I sent in word for him to tuck away the ball. Here he went again, this time ducking and dodging. We were lucky he didn't lose the ball. By now I was on my hands and knees on the sidelines, pounding on the turf and yelling, "George, fall on the damn ball!"

Across the turf came his answer. "But Coach, it'll hurt my rushing average!"

That team won five games, the most yet. By the time the 1971 season rolled around, we were ready to stand up and be counted. The outstanding freshmen from the previous year were now sophomores, and for the first time we had the kind of experience, speed, and depth that was required to compete in the strongest football conference in America at that time. We went 8–3, and the three losses came at the hands of the teams that finished number one, number two, and number three in the nation that year: Nebraska, Oklahoma, and Colorado.

Iowa State had never been to a bowl, so you can imagine the tension surrounding the last game of the season with Oklahoma State at Ames. By this time we were drawing full house crowds of about 33,000, compared to an average of less than 18,000 in the '60s.

We won the coin toss, and I took the wind instead of the ball. I began to wonder if I had made a mistake when Oklahoma State returned to the forty-yard line and then made a first down at midfield on the first play from scrimmage. But we knocked the ball loose on the next play, and on our first snap Carlson hit Ike Harris for a fifty-five-yard touchdown. We won the game, 54–0, and I have never seen a more excited football crowd. They stayed for more than an hour after the game, and the band kept playing. It was announced that we would be going to the Sun Bowl; that was one of the happiest days of my life, right up there with winning the Duck River Valley Conference championship in 1950.

We played Louisiana State in the Sun Bowl. Our players were on edge, and so was I. Usually I calm down a little once the whistle blows, but my heart pounded full blast all through the first half. We lost, 30–15, to a good LSU team, with Bert Jones at quarterback. I didn't feel that we did ourselves justice, as we were a little intimidated and suffered from stagefright.

The 1972 team was a disappointment. We had almost everyone back from the good team of the previous year, but we didn't keep them for long. That team was hit by more injuries to more key players than any time I've ever coached, except for the 1980 Tennessee team. During the season we lost Amundson, Krepfle, Strachan, Harris, and several other regulars for long periods of time. We also lost some close games, finishing the season at 5–5–1. Ties usually aren't very exciting, but that one was—both during and after the game.

I had finally won approval for the stadium enlargement, which was to be done between the 1972 and 1973 seasons. A new member of the athletics council, Dr. Hadwiger, was speaking out very strongly against the expansion, however. On the day before the Nebraska game at Ames, Jim Moakler of the *Des Moines Register* did a full page piece on Dr. Hadwiger and the reasons he didn't think we should have a new stadium. There wasn't much about the Nebraska game, just the controversial story on the overemphasis on athletics.

We played a heck of a game against Nebraska. In it we used a pass play suggested by my dad, who had come to Ames for the game, sending the tight end out twenty yards over the middle and sending our great wide receiver, Willie Jones, deep on a post route. The deep man had to cover one or the other, and Amundson hit him for a thirty-yard touchdown to tie the score at 23–23 with about twenty seconds left. The crowd erupted, and it took several minutes to clear the field. Then, in the worst anticlimax I've ever seen, our young placekicker, Tom Gadjean, who later became a great one, missed the extra point that would have won the game against the defending national champions.

You can imagine our feelings. We were heartbroken. As I walked into the dressing room, Jim Moakler stopped me and said, "What do you think of Dr. Hadwiger's statement about the stadium?" From my point of view, the timing couldn't have been worse.

"If I had him here right now, I'd punch him in the nose!" I said.

That was a purely emotional reaction because I have never been a fist fighter.

I never dreamed that Jim would use that quote, but on page one of the Big Peach section of the *Des Moines Register* the next day, right under the streamer on the game, was a big headline: "MAJORS THREATENS PROFESSOR."

As soon as I saw it, I turned to Mary Lynn and said, "Honey, could I possibly have been that stupid?"

What I should have done was to call Dr. Hadwiger and apologize right then. I had nothing against him. He had his ideas, and I had mine, and that's what this country is supposed to be about. However, I didn't really know him; he was new on the council; and I thought I'd just see if things would die down on their own.

They didn't. On Tuesday night I got a call at home from a member of the faculty council. "Coach Majors," he said. "We have voted to censure you for your remarks threatening one of our professors. Do you have anything to say?"

"No. I don't know what the censure means. I have had no hearing, and I don't know what the charge is," I answered.

The newspapers and national wire services picked up on the story, and ran with it pretty good. I was mad by this time and got stubborn and bullheaded, refusing to tell anyone my side of the story.

Several days later I was in the office when my secretary came in and told me that Dr. Hadwiger was there to see me. I was embarrassed, and I think he was, too, for we both started apologizing at the same time. He said, "My students have been giving me a hard time about this. They like football, and I certainly don't have anything against you or your program."

I told him I was embarrassed by what had happened, and that I had been very rash in what I had said after the game. We parted on good terms.

A couple of years later when I was at Pittsburgh, an Iowa State professor, Harold W. Davey, persuaded the faculty council to withdraw the censure from its records on the grounds that I was never given a hearing and that there was no justification for it.

Bob Devaney of Nebraska also had to do a little squirming after that game. We had used a quick huddle play for a big gain, and on his Sunday television show the announcer asked Bob what he thought it was. "It looked like a bunch of farmers going to a picnic," he said. Bob heard from the farmers, a bunch of them, but he was so well liked that he was able to handle it without making any enemies.

We were 5–3–1 going into the last two games, and the Liberty Bowl invited us to Memphis to play Georgia Tech. They could have backed out of the deal when we lost both of those games, but the president, Herbie Hunt, a former Kentucky player and personal friend, stuck with us. He was criticized for his decision, but it turned out to be one of the best games in Liberty Bowl history. Tech beat us, 31–30, and we missed a two point conversion try at the end of the game.

That was my last game at Iowa State. The next day I caught an early morning flight to Pittsburgh. There it was announced that I was to become the new head coach of the University of Pittsburgh Panthers.

-25-

Pittsburgh Hires a Coach

Early in 1972 I had made up my mind to leave Iowa State once the season was finished. Clay Stapleton had left a couple of years earlier to take the athletic director job at Florida State, and I did not always agree philosophically with his successor, Lou McCullough. But those matters did not weigh that heavily on my decision. The two big reasons were Oklahoma and Nebraska. It was clear that it always would be difficult to compete with those rich, established programs. As Dean Knudson, a friend and Iowa State patron, said, "We grow corn in Iowa; they grow oil in Oklahoma."

I interviewed with several schools during the last two years at Iowa State. One night in 1971 I went to sleep feeling that Bobby Dodd had assured me that I was to be named the head coach at Georgia Tech the next day; but when the phone rang in the morning, it was Coach Dodd's assistant athletic director, John McKenna, telling me that Bill Fulcher had gotten the job. Southern Methodist, Texas A & M, Texas Tech, Baylor, Rice, Michigan State, and Purdue were among the schools that contacted me; some made offers, and some did not. I don't think it's very considerate to make it public when you turn down a job, and I kept the offers to myself, with one exception. Rice offered me the dual coach-athletic director position, and when I declined, the president asked me to announce that I had refused it. He wanted his board to know he had offered the position to me.

Pittsburgh had contacted me in October of 1972. Bob Miller, a booster who was very close to the Pittsburgh program, called several times during the season asking me to visit the school. I had no notion of going to Pittsburgh. It was a big city, and I was a small town boy. But Bob was persistent, and finally I asked my brother Joe, whose judgment I trust as much as anyone I know, if he would do some reconnoitering for me. He spent a couple of days at Pittsburgh, meeting with the chancellor, the athletic director, and other key people, then came out to Ames for the Nebraska game.

"Those people are ready to make a move in the right direction," he said. "The locker room is terrible, and the stadium needs repairs. But they really want to get competitive, and they've got an athletic director who will stand behind you. I think that you are the right man for Pittsburgh at this time."

As the Liberty Bowl game drew near, it came down to Pitt and Purdue. I would have taken the Purdue job and probably would have gotten it if Alex Agasse, an old Boilermaker himself, hadn't decided at the last moment to leave Northwestern for his alma mater. So I visited Pittsburgh for interviews. On the day of the Liberty Bowl game I told Cas Myslinski, the athletic director, that he had a new coach.

I have been a little naive in contract matters. Money has never been a big consideration in any of the moves I've made. At Pittsburgh I never got around to mentioning salary until I already had agreed to take the job, and at both Pittsburgh and Tennessee I didn't sign a contract for several weeks. The Pitt contract was for $30,000. I know now that it was a pretty modest amount, and if I had to do it over again I would try to drive a little harder bargain. But my financial situation improved over my four years there, and of course there was money from a television show. If I was underpaid, I wasn't smart enough to know it.

The first thing I told the Pittsburgh committee was that the school was getting the short end of the stick in football scholarships. "You're getting beaten by numbers," I said.

That was in reference to the agreement the school had with the other Big Four schools—Penn State, West Virginia, and Syracuse—that called for a limit of twenty-five scholarships per year. This was during the time the NCAA had no limits, and Big Eight teams, for instance, were awarding forty-five scholarships per year. Pitt had already decided to get out of the Big Four agreement, but they had not set a new number. I suggested fifty per year, and the committee agreed.

I guess most football people know by now that we signed eighty-three players that first year. I have taken a lot of criticism for that. I have even been blamed for the NCAA limit of thirty scholarships per year and the total of ninety-five, which went into effect the following year. The fact is that we signed that many because both Cas Myslinski and I had gotten wind of the thirty/ninety-five rule, and Pittsburgh's player stockpile was so low that if we didn't move right then we might never be able to catch up.

I had brought most of my Iowa State staff with me, and they were great recruiters. They fanned out all over everywhere— Pennsylvania, Ohio, New Jersey, Florida, Georgia—and when we approached the agreed school limit, I went to see the athletic director. I told him it looked as if we were going past fifty. He didn't say we couldn't. When it reached sixty, I went back to him.

"Let's go see the chancellor," he suggested.

Dr. Wesley Posvar, like Cas Myslinski, is a West Point graduate. He also was a Rhodes scholar who, I was told, had finished cadet training with the highest scholastic marks since Douglas MacArthur. He is a brilliant man and a most interesting individual. His wife is a former Metropolitan Opera star, and one of the great thrills Mary Lynn and I had during our stay in Pittsburgh was seeing and hearing her perform in *The Barber of Seville*. It was the first opera I ever had seen, and I surprised myself by enjoying it.

Apprised of the scholarship situation, Dr. Posvar simply said, "Can you handle it?"

"Yes, sir," said Cas. So we moved the limit up to eighty-three signees before we stopped.

I have never felt any guilt about signing that many football players. It was not in violation of the rules, and I did it with the knowledge and approval of my athletic director and chancellor. It was easy for people at those schools whose football programs were on solid ground to throw rocks at us, but Pittsburgh had gone 1–9, 3–8, 1–9, and 1–10 over the past four seasons. The Panthers had been beaten so badly in some games that the story had it that the clock at Pitt Stadium was kept running during timeouts during the second half. I don't know if that was true, but it does give a pretty good picture of the state of the program at the time.

It is my opinion that we could not have rebuilt Pitt football without that kind of dramatic action, because the thirty/ninety-five rule came in the very next year. Actually, we did not get a lot of great players among that first group, but we did get some good ones. They were good kids and when I left there four years later, forty-seven of them were still on scholarship. Of course, since Tony Dorsett was part of the class, it was a good recruiting year by any standard.

My fears of not being able to adjust to living in Pittsburgh were quickly dispelled. Although it is a great eastern city with all the cosmopolitan features that one would expect, I found that it had a small town flavor. Most of the people were blue collar workers, very loyal to family and friends. For the first time in my life, I was exposed to a variety of ethnic groups. In time I became a regular member of a golf group of Pitt boosters that included insurance executive Eddie Ifft, of German extraction; industrialist Bob Casey, a wild Irishman; my dentist Pat Cupelli, an Italian-American; television executive John Connemikes, a handsome Greek; and contractor Joe Massaro, another Italian-American. That was Pittsburgh and I learned to love it.

When Mary Lynn finally was able to bring the children from Ames after about five months, we found a great house in Fox Chapel, not more than fifteen minutes away from the office. It was just what we wanted, a traditional two-story frame house, and it quickly became an oasis. No matter how many troubles I had on my mind, when I reached Fox Chapel they faded away.

Mary Lynn and I have enjoyed every place where we have lived, and it was tough to leave Ames. There aren't any better people in the world than Iowans. They don't measure you by how much money you have, but by what you are. It was the most democratic place I've known. There never seemed to be any social lines drawn; anyone could belong to the country club, for instance. Also, Ames was one of the cleanest towns I've ever seen, and it had a very low crime rate.

As we left Ames, Mary Lynn said, "No matter where we go, nothing will ever top this experience."

That was true, but some more excitement was on its way.

So while it would seem that we moved 180 degrees from the middle-America small town to the eastern big city, we found the same friendly spirit under the surface at both places. People are people everywhere, if you just give them a chance.

·26·

The Incomparable Tony Dorsett

"Tony Dorsett is the best football player in Pennsylvania," claimed Foge Fazio, "and one of the best in the country."

I had retained Foge from the old Pitt staff as recruiting coordinator, and I had asked him who was our number one prospect.

There were no NCAA limits on the number of recruiting visits then, and we kept the path hot between Pittsburgh and the Aliquippa area, where Tony had just finished his career for Hopewell High School. I probably saw him twenty times, and Jackie Sherrill forty, before we signed him. Some of those visits were just a matter of dropping by for a few minutes, but we didn't let the trail grow cold. Tony had been recruited by more than 100 schools, but he had narrowed his choices down to Pitt, Ohio State, Penn State, and Colorado. It was a big day for our program when we signed him. At the same time, we also got a fine defensive end in his teammate, Ed Wilamowski.

When I came to Pittsburgh, the cupboard was so close to being bare that we had a hard time getting enough football players to play a spring game in 1973. We had been working in units in practice, and when I saw the squad divided into two teams that day, I turned to Joe Avezzano and said, "When is the rest of the team coming out?"

"You're looking at it," he answered.

We had about fifty players dressed out that day. Our captain, Rod Kirby, had to miss practice because his grandfather had died; this left one of the teams without anybody at his linebacking position. One of our part-time coaches, Keith Schroeder, had been a good linebacker for us at Iowa State, and he suddenly found himself reactivated. Jackie Sherrill made him play the whole game. Keith was young and single and had been out late the previous night. Toward the end of the game, he began to beg to come out of the game, but Jackie said, "You've got to suck it up, Schroeder. Fourth quarter!"

We had two good tailbacks going into spring practice, and none coming out of it. Mel Howard, a transfer from Texas A & M, was the star of the spring game, but he never was able to become academically eligible and never played a down for us. And Mike Mihalik, a good, solid, hardworking kid, tore up a knee and never played again.

I was pretty discouraged and called Bob Dillon back in Des Moines. I told him that I didn't even have a tailback. "When it's darkest," he said, "that's when you can see the stars."

He was right. I saw one of the brightest stars in football in action during July in the "Big 33" game at Hershey between the Pennsylvania and Ohio high school all-stars. I was sitting at one end of the press box with John Connemikes and Dean Billick, our sports information director. Joe Paterno was down at the other end. The game was barely under way when Dorsett made a spectacular run, like none I ever had seen. Hemmed in at one sideline, he reversed his field, changed speeds, stopped and started again, and finally broke away for a touchdown.

John and Dean started yelling, and I gave them a little nudge to quieten them down. I didn't want Paterno to hear us celebrating. But when I got home that night and closed the door behind me, I let out a yell.

"Yahoo! I've got a tailback!"

Tony was a good kid, a quiet young man who didn't talk a lot. He came from a nice family; his dad was a steel worker. He always accepted the disciplines of football; and as much as any player I've ever seen, he always was aware of the game situation. He knew where he was on the field, and he knew what needed to be done. He made a tremendous sudden impact on the team in our first scrimmage that fall.

We had come out of spring practice with what looked like a pretty good defense and a very questionable offense. In the first scrimmage that fall, on his very first play, Tony got the ball on a sprint draw, and BOOM! He was through the hole and digging.

When I saw him break the line of scrimmage, I took off after him, running along the sidelines. Eighty yards later he crossed the goal line. He scored four touchdowns that day.

After practice I found the defensive coaches huddled in a sort of prayer meeting. "We've got problems," said Jackie Sherrill.

"I may be wrong, but I don't think we have a problem," I answered. "I think that what we've got is one of the great running backs in football. Tony Dorsett is going to make a lot of defenses look bad before he's through."

That first year at Pitt wasn't easy. It was a time of change, and change always is difficult. The players have to adjust to a new staff, and the coaches have to establish discipline. The team must always come first, and those players who put themselves ahead of the team either have to adapt or leave. We had some players leave in the spring, and then again in preseason practice in the fall. Thanks to our big freshman class, however, our numbers had grown from about 50 to 140.

We took the team to a camp just outside of Johnstown, Pennsylvania, and we worked them very hard. They badly needed conditioning, so for the first two years at Pitt we had them on two conditioning drills a day. Because we had so many pulled muscles in the second season, I cut down on the two-a-day drills and also shortened the length of practices. You learn by your mistakes in this business, as in any other.

I am a little shy about claiming to have made a lot of bright moves as a coach, but I did do one intelligent thing shortly after arriving at Pitt. A young man named Tim Kerin impressed me with his enthusiasm and dedication as assistant trainer; I recommended that he be made head trainer. Tim has been with me ever since, fourteen seasons now; and I'm convinced that he is the premier football trainer in the country.

When I arrived at Pitt, the school had no weight room, just one Universal machine. With Tim's help, by fall we had an up-to-date facility ready. At first, the locker room looked like Jock Sutherland's teams had dressed there, but Cas Myslinski, the athletic director, had agreed to have new facilities for the players ready for the fall. We had the facilities as promised, but the coaches still had to dress and shower in rather primitive quarters. I didn't think that was so important. The players have to come first on a football team.

I went to great care and expense in ordering new uniforms. To me, that is always a top priority. A team's outward appearance, the way it looks to the public, is a very important thing. With these improvements, and through the work of a great group of assistant coaches, we were able to communicate our message of pride and enthusiasm to the team. By the time those freshmen were seniors, we had absolutely no disciplinary problems on the Pittsburgh football squad.

However, there were problems at first. One of the players who had left the squad, fullback Lou Cecconi, had criticized our practice procedures. I went on a television program one night, and the host, Sam Novar, suddenly waylaid me. "I understand you run a brutal program," he said.

I was angry, but before I could answer, the other two sportscasters on the panel came to my defense. "Have you been to the Pitt practices?" they asked him. When he admitted he hadn't, they said, "You're being unfair."

Then I defended myself. After all, football is a very physical game and I regard myself as a hard-nose coach, but there is no place for brutality in the game as far as I am concerned. I also made it very clear that there was no room on a team of mine for people who wouldn't put the team first and who wouldn't get in the kind of shape I demanded.

The public response was on my side, and the station got several letters protesting the question. Later on, Sam Novar and I became friends, and he and I played a few rounds of golf together. He hadn't meant to be unfair; he was just being aggressive.

We also got some unfavorable publicity when one of our players was involved in an altercation on campus. Tom Perko, a big defensive lineman, was the toughest guy on the team. The players had enough sense not to mess with him, but there always is somebody who wants to try to punch Jack Dempsey in the nose. One day a Pitt student challenged Tom and wound up in a hospital. It wasn't Tom's fault at all; he didn't start the fight, but it got in the papers and stayed there for days.

I learned a long time ago not to worry too much about things I can't control. I can't control the press, and I wouldn't want to if I could. I have had some great friends in the newspaper, radio, and television fields. They have their jobs to do, and I have mine; and our interests don't always coincide.

Unpleasant things sometimes seem to be overpublicized, but I tell my players that we have to expect that because the good things get overpublicized, too. We just happen to be involved in something that interests the public, and our actions, good or bad, are always going to get a lot of attention.

✦27✦

Panthers on the Prowl

One of my most pleasant surprises as a head coach was the 7–7 tie my first Pittsburgh team played with Georgia in the opening game of the 1973 season.

We weren't supposed to have a chance going into the game. Pitt had been 1–10 the previous year, and the game was being played in Athens, Between the Hedges, where Georgia always seems to have a big home field advantage. It was an extremely hot day, even for Georgia in early September, and our tough conditioning program paid off for us. As the game progressed, our team seemed to get stronger. We almost beat them, but Carson Long, our freshman kicker who later broke every record in the books, missed a field goal from inside the thirty-five-yard line near the end of the game.

The Georgia fans booed the Bulldog players as they left the field, the first time I had ever heard a crowd boo its own team in college football. However, I only had to wait one week to hear it again.

The next Saturday we played Baylor at Pitt Stadium. I don't think anybody in Pittsburgh had ever heard of Baylor. I knew we were going up against a good team, but I guess I didn't do a good job of getting that across to the players. We played terribly and lost, 19–9; and some of the fans booed us as we left the field.

Two or three days later I was having lunch downtown with a friend, when he said, "I hate to tell you this, but a lot of the people in Section L didn't think we looked very good on offense."

I hate it when people start out by saying, "I hate to tell you this, but. . . ." If they hate to tell me, they just shouldn't do it.

I said, "From where I was, our offense looked a lot worse than that. I tell you what I'm going to do. I'm going to put you in charge of Section L, and if you hear any more complaints, you handle them. Don't bring them to me!"

Dorsett had his first great game the following Saturday at Northwestern. He ran for something like 265 yards on thirty-nine carries and had a sixty-five-yard touchdown run. It amazed me how he could carry the ball that much and stay fresh, especially early in his career when he weighed only 160 pounds. From that day on he was a major force in college football. We went on to finish 6–4–1 that season, losing to a great Arizona State team that had Danny White at quarterback in the Fiesta Bowl, 28–7.The Football Writers of America voted me national Coach of the Year for 1973. That's an honor that would have overwhelmed me at any time, but this one was especially meaningful. My dad was voted small college Coach of the Year for his work at Sewanee. It is the only time a father and son have been honored in the same season. I was every bit as proud for my dad as I was for myself.

Tony Dorsett wasn't our only fine football player at Pittsburgh. Al Romano was a great nose guard, an All-American in his senior year. The first practice sessions in his freshman year were almost too much for Al; he was discouraged, like many players in their freshman year, and the other coaches and I managed to talk him out of leaving.

Al was a strikingly handsome Italian fellow, with dark eyes and heavy eyebrows and a black mustache. Women from eight to eighty were attracted to him. Mary Lynn and Jan Madden were talking to Al's dad one day, and Mary Lynn said, "Mr. Romano, Al's not only a good football player, he's also a very good-looking guy."

Mr. Romano, who had a lot of charm of his own, answered, "You sow tomatoes, you grow tomatoes."

Don Parrish, a black kid from Tallahassee, Florida, was a strong defensive tackle. The other players called him "Chocolate Chip." The same year Joe Avezzano brought in a player from his old Miami High school, linebacker Cecil Johnson. Cecil was something of a free spirit, but he was a terrific player who has been a star for the Tampa Bay Buccaneers for several years. I had to stay on top of Parrish and Johnson to be sure they did their school work. Once I called them in and asked them if they were keeping up with the books. "We haven't missed a class, Coach," said Parrish.

Later that day I was talking to the academic counselor and mentioned that I was happy that Don and Cecil hadn't missed a class. "Haven't missed a class?" he said. "They haven't been to one in several days!"

We had several other outstanding players. Randy Holloway was an All-American defensive tackle. Jim Corbett was an All-East tight end, and Gordon Jones was a fine receiver. Willie Taylor, an outstanding flanker, had played high school football under an old Tennessee man, Al Rotella, in New Jersey. Arnie Weatherington, linebacker and a team captain, and fullback Elliott Walker were two more of Avezzano's fine Miami recruits. We had two superlative quarterbacks, Matt Cavanaugh and Robert Haygood; and both our kickers, Carson Long and punter Larry Swider, were regulars all four years.

Our big games were with Penn State, Notre Dame, and West Virginia. Penn State was the reigning eastern power and a natural in-state rival. With all its mystique and tradition, Notre Dame is a big rival for anybody the Irish play. And the Pitt-West Virginia rivalry is like the feud between the Hatfields and the McCoys.

Dorsett always had great days against Notre Dame, with the exception of his sophomore year when he was coming off an injury and wasn't quite himself. I think he ended up with over 700 yards against Notre Dame in four games. The 1975 Notre Dame game at Pitt Stadium may have been his greatest. He rushed for 305 yards that day, scored three touchdowns, and went fifty-nine yards with the only pass he caught. We won, 34–20, the first time Pitt had beaten Notre Dame in twelve years.

Penn State was the toughest nut to crack. Joe Paterno had, and still has, a great program going. His teams always play smart, basic football and very seldom beat themselves. That's the kind of background I came from, under the influence of my dad, Bowden Wyatt, and General Neyland. Consequently, I've always been a great admirer of Joe Paterno.

In each of my first three seasons at Pitt, we led Penn State at half time, only to end up losing at the end. The first two games weren't as hard to accept since Penn State had a better team than we did, and I knew it. But in 1975 I thought we were just about as good as they were, and our 7–6 loss was about as disappointing as any I've ever experienced.

Our great kicker, Carson Long, missed three field goals from close range, and he was absolutely devastated. I've never seen a football player torn up more about a bad game. His wife had a baby that night, but even that couldn't pull him out of his depression. He was still hanging his head when fall practice started in 1976.

Carson and I had always been close. We had recruited him out of Ashland, Pennsylvania, after George Boutselis, who had moved from Iowa State with me, told me that he was the best high school kicker in the country that year. I didn't think all that moping was doing anybody any good, so I got on him after an indifferent scrimmage.

"Carson, I want you to quit feeling sorry for yourself," I said. And then went on to other things.

The next day he came to see me. "Coach Majors," he said, "I don't appreciate you getting on me like that. I'm going to do my best, but I just want you to know that you're not my friend anymore."

"Oh, yes, I am your friend," I replied. "I care very much about you, but if you keep on feeling sorry for yourself and hanging your head, you will lose your friends and people will stop caring for you. You owe it to yourself and the team to put the past behind you."

Carson was cool to me for a couple of weeks, but then he got caught up in the excitement of the season. He had a great senior year and has stayed in touch with me more closely than any other member of the championship team.

We finished 7–4 in 1975 and beat a good Kansas team, 33–14, in the Sun Bowl. Almost the entire team was coming back for the next season, and we knew that 1976 could be something special.

But we didn't know how special it would be.

·28·

National Championship

Before the 1976 season, I did something I had never done previously and haven't done again since. I knew that we had the makings of an extraordinary team, possibly even a national champion, and I felt that the only thing that could deny us a great season would be incapacitating injuries to key players. So I decided that there would be no full speed contact for our final pre-season scrimmage. It was such a radical departure from my background that I called Frank Broyes and Darrell Royal to see how they reacted to it. They both liked the idea.

While all other practice routines remained the same as they had been, in this scrimmage the defensive players were to make the initial hit on tackles and then stop, instead of taking people to the ground. I was uncertain about whether it was the right step to take, but when I reviewed the films of our game-type workout eight days before the season opener, I was very pleased. Our timing and execution were excellent.

You have to have a special kind of team before you can try something that extreme and make it work, but this was a special team. They were mostly juniors and seniors and had played together for so long that full speed contact wasn't going to help them much anyway. That they were exceptionally well-conditioned certainly helped, too.

We had been scheduled to open the season at home against Louisville, but ABC-TV asked us to switch dates and play at Notre Dame instead. Louisville had an open date on the day we were supposed to play the Irish, and my old friend Vince Gibson, the Louisville coach, agreed to the change. That set up one of the most dynamic opening games in which I've ever participated—Pittsburgh at Notre Dame.

Tony had had his greatest day ever against the Irish the previous season, and Notre Dame was thirsting for revenge. Their players had the letter *D*, for Dorsett, drawn on their foreheads with ashes. Paul Hornung, who did the Notre Dame telecasts with Lindsey Nelson, said in a pregame broadcast that there was no way that Tony could have a 200-yard day. The Irish were gunning for him this time. I was even more convinced that they were out to get him when we worked out on Friday afternoon. The grass was shoetop high, not the ideal turf for a back who runs the forty in 4.3 seconds.

"This reminds me of a Kansas wheat field," I told our staff. The Notre Dame people insisted it was mowed to standard level, and that was good enough for me.

Notre Dame took the opening kickoff, kept the ball for over seven minutes, and stuck it in our end zone. The crowd responded with noise that was deafening. It became even louder after they kicked off through the end zone, against the wind at that. On our first play from scrimmage, a counter dive with Dorsett carrying, our right tackle, Joe Stone, jumped offsides. We were moving fast, all right, but in the wrong direction.

"Run the same play," I told our quarterback coach, Bill Cox. "It's too early to try anything fancy." Ordinarily I let the assistant responsible call his own plays, but in this instance I wanted to make sure that we stayed with the game plan.

The next play was one that Mary Lynn still says was the most dramatic she has ever seen. Dorsett got the handoff, bounced off a linebacker three or four yards past the line of scrimmage, picked up some blockers, and high-tailed it about sixty-five yards to somewhere around the Notre Dame twenty-yard line. Suddenly the crowd was quiet.

Now we were knocking at Notre Dame's door. We scored a few plays later, and from then on it was all Pitt. We won, 31–10. Dorsett gained 181 yards, and if I hadn't pulled the first team early in the fourth quarter he easily would have gone past Hornung's 200-yard limit.

By this time everybody we played had begun to overload the defense, bringing the weak safety up to take on Dorsett man-for-man, more or less. Consequently, for the Duke game we put in an option pass series to our veer offense to take advantage of that. They managed to hold Tony to forty yards in the first half, but Matt Cavanaugh was able to fire three touchdown passes. After Matt loosened them up, Tony had a strong second half and we won, 44–31.

The Louisville game was notable for two reasons. Our crowds had grown steadily, from an average of about 19,000 in 1973 to about 45,000 in 1976. I wanted a big turnout for the Louisville game, so I preached a sermon on my Sunday television show.

"We need the band to play a peppy song for the offense and something militant for the defense," I said. "If the fans will hold up red and green "Stop and Go' flags when those units take the field, we'll have them ready for them at the stadium."

I had made a rash promise, and now I had to deliver. The campus community jumped on the bandwagon. The Chancellor even called to see what he could do to help. Henry Lee Parker, who had joined our staff as my administrative assistant, started out in quest of red and green material to use for making the flags. He called all over Pennsylvania, and finally on Thursday he found enough at a cloth shop in Altoona. We sent a truck up to get it, and then had volunteer helpers cut the cloth. They used scissors and razor blades and meat cleavers, anything that had a sharp edge, and we got the flags ready.

Unfortunately, it poured down rain on Saturday, but a big crowd turned out anyway. Those great Pittsburgh fans waved our red and green flags throughout the game.

We had the game well under control, 27–0, in the first half when Cavanaugh was injured. I knew he was hurt badly before Tim Kerin ran onto the field. After they had brought Matt to the sidelines, he said to me, "I'm afraid it's a broken leg."

It turned out that a small bone had been broken in his leg, and we faced the immediate future without a proven quarterback. Bob Haygood, Matt's backup and a good one, had suffered a knee injury earlier and was out for the season. Despite all my precautions, it appeared that injuries to one key position might destroy our hopes for a great season.

We had two other quarterbacks, neither of whom had played in a game. Tom Yewcic was a walk-on senior from Johnstown, Pennsylvania. His dad was a coach, and an uncle of the same name had been a fine quarterback at Michigan State; so he had a solid football background. The second quarterback was Woody Jackson, a very quick freshman, who was a good runner but couldn't throw well. We used Yewcic the rest of the Louisville game and hung on to win, 27–7.

Looking closely at both of them in practice the following week, I was not impressed by Yewcic physically, but I liked the way he handled himself. After Wednesday's workout, I asked, "How about it, Tom?"

"Coach, I can handle it," he said.

I gave him a scholarship before we started him against Miami that Saturday. I figured if he was going to take on that responsibility, he deserved what the others were getting. It turned out like one of those Broadway shows where the unknown understudy stands in for the big star and steals the show. When he completed his first pass attempt, a little dink for four or five yards, the crowd gave him a standing ovation. Tom ran the offense flawlessly. Dorsett gained 230 yards, and we beat Miami, 36-19.

College football doesn't have any finer moments than when a dedicated, hard-working athlete comes off the bench to help his team reach its goals. Nine years later, at Tennessee, I would be privileged to watch Daryl Dickey do the same thing when he took over for the injured Tony Robinson at midseason and led us to the Southeastern Conference title and the Sugar Bowl championship.

Dorsett broke the all-time college career rushing record against Navy at Annapolis. We had the game under control, 31–0, and I didn't want to run up the score against George Welch, whom I respect highly. Everybody knew that Tony was getting close to the record; the announcer kept the crowd up-to-date every time he carried the ball. I told the players on the first unit that, record or not, this was their last series.

Tony was ten yards short of the record when we moved past midfield. I told Yewcic to run the option and try to get Tony outside. Tony broke three tackles and went forty-four yards for a touchdown.

The game turned into a mob scene. The players ran out onto the field, and nobody except the assistant coaches and I were left at our bench. A mass of human bodies wearing Pittsburgh blue and gold celebrated in the end zone for several minutes. In a great display of sportsmanship, the corps of midshipmen escorted Tony to the Navy student section, which stood cheering for several minutes.

Syracuse gave us our biggest scare that season. We led, 20–13, in the third quarter, and they had the ball with third and one to go inside our twenty. We stopped them for no gain on two consecutive plays, with Al Romano leading the defensive charge. We then went on to win, 23–13.

With Cavanaugh back, we had a rather easy win over Army at Pitt Stadium. During the game, the fans' attention was focused as much on the public address system as on the field. We went into the game ranked number two in the nation behind Michigan. The Wolverines were playing Purdue that day, and Purdue was winning. The loudspeaker was hooked up to the closing moments of that game, and when they counted down the last ten seconds, the crowd went wild.

My friend Eddie Ifft had long taken delight at Purdue wins over Notre Dame. The next morning he always would give his Notre Dame friends an early telephone call. Without any preamble, he would chant, "Purdue, Purdue, Purdue, Purdue!" in staccatto fashion and then hang up.

On the morning after Purdue beat Michigan, I dialed Eddie's number. 'Purdue, Purdue, Purdue, Purdue!" I hollered. And I hung up.

Pitt football had moved onto the top shelf. Ranked number one and boasting a sure-fire Heisman Trophy winner, we began to attract the national media. On the day Tony decided to change the pronunciation of his name, Phyllis George was on campus with a CBS team to do a special on us.

"Coach, what do you think about Tony wanting to be called Dor-SETT?" she asked.

"That's fine with me," I answered. "If it would help us win, I'd be glad to change my name to Ma-JORS!"

A hard-earned win over West Virginia set the stage for the season's climax, the big game with Penn State at Three Rivers Stadium in Pittsburgh. As if that were not enough to keep me occupied, Bill Battle resigned at Tennessee on the Monday before we were to play the Nittany Lions on Friday night. I had to keep away from the inevitable speculation that I knew would follow, and I told my secretary that I wouldn't return any calls from the press that week. I did talk with Ben Byrd of the *Knoxville Journal* and with two or three other writers of long acquaintance, but I didn't have a lot to tell them, except that I had not been in contact with the Tennessee people. I had determined to put the Penn State game behind us before talking to anybody.

We had not been able to beat Penn State in the three previous seasons. I knew we were the stronger team this time, but I also realized that we would have to clear a psychological barrier if we were going to beat them. When one team gets the upper hand over a period of years in these old rivalries, it becomes increasingly difficult for the losers to break the ice. We later encountered the same situation at Tennessee with Alabama.

To deal with the Penn State stumbling block, I vowed that I would never again be so overconservative against Penn State. As Bob Dillon has told me so often, "When you have the troops—Attack! Attack! Attack!" This time I had the troops.

We played Penn State on a cold, drizzly Friday night; ABC televised it nationally. It was the first time in four years that we hadn't led them at half time; we were tied, 7–7, at intermission. Joe Paterno's teams are always hard to play; he is shrewd and basic and never beats himself. He always seemed to come up with something new on defense against us, so we put in a new offensive wrinkle for the game. We lined up in an unbalanced line with Dorsett at fullback, and Tony broke open for a forty-yard touchdown run in the third quarter. We went on to win, 24–7.

Pittsburgh was a happy town that night. A lot of the Majors family was there for the game, and we had some good friends over at the house to help us celebrate. Eddie Ifft had given us a bottle of champagne after every game Pittsburgh had won, and I had told Mary Lynn that nobody was touching a drop of it until we beat Penn State. It took four years, but we popped the corks that night.

We were left in a commanding position to deal with the bowls—number one in the nation and the Heisman Trophy winner to boot. Because of my background in the Big Eight Conference, I had leaned toward the Orange Bowl earlier. I wanted a crack at Oklahoma or Nebraska or another of the teams that had made life hard for us at Iowa State, but as the bowl picture developed, the Sugar Bowl became the natural choice. It was one of those rare years when the Big Eight had no team with anything better than an 8–3 record, and I felt that we needed to beat somebody with better statistics to solidify our claims to the national championship. In this case I thought the Sugar Bowl was our best bet. Georgia was 10–1, but I felt we had a considerably stronger team.

Charlie Gluck and Henry Bodenheimer represented the Sugar Bowl at the Penn State game. There was a pep rally that Thursday night, and the crowd was so thick and boisterous that the campus police had to take Mary Lynn, Charlie, Henry, and me away in a paddy wagon to escape the crush. As we were riding along, Mary Lynn called our attention to the weather.

"Look, it's starting to snow."

"Honey, that's not snow. It's sugar," Charlie drawled in his down home Southern accent.

I had to spend a lot of early December commuting between Pittsburgh and Tennessee, but I made up my mind that I would not let the new developments interfere with four years of hard work and the chance at a national championship. I had received the national Coach of the Year award for a second time, and I wanted to cap off the season with the very best possible effort for all those wonderful Pittsburgh players, supporters, and fans who had been so good to us.

We took the team to Biloxi, Mississippi, on December 20. We were able to avoid outside distractions and get in a good week of hard practice before moving into New Orleans on December 26. I gave the players a lot of freedom, which always has been my policy on bowl trips. They handled it like the responsible people I knew they were, and we were ready to play Georgia on New Year's Day.

Georgia tried some of the same defensive tactics that we had faced during the season. They loaded up the defensive secondary to stop Dorsett, and Cavanaugh threw for about 180 yards in the first half, including a touchdown pass to Jones. Tony broke loose in the second half and wound up with more than 200 yards. We won the Sugar Bowl, 27–3.

What a happy memory it is to have been a part of Pittsburgh's national championship team of 1976! It was a team without a real weakness, one of the greatest college teams of the last two decades. I realized even then that I was a very fortunate man. Few people in our profession ever have the experience of working with a team that good.

I didn't have long to savor the taste of victory. I was going home again.

·29·

Back to Tennessee

The rumors surrounding my move from Pittsburgh to Tennessee all had one thing in common. They were wrong.

Some said the deal had been cut for weeks. Others claimed I had been talking with Tennessee officials on and off at various places. Yet others said athletic director Bob Woodruff and I did not like each other. Et cetera, et cetera, et cetera. I know there always will be rumors surrounding football and the changing of head coaches, and there is nothing any of us can do about them, but I guess it's time to set the record straight.

I had not talked with any Tennessee official about the head coaching job during the 1976 season. The only time I ever had expressed an interest in returning to Tennessee was in December of 1969, when it became rather well known that Doug Dickey was leaving to go to Florida. I was at Iowa State at the time, and Mary Lynn and I went to Jacksonville to see my brother Bob play for Tennessee in the Gator Bowl game with Florida. While I was there, I visited with some of the Tennessee people, including Tom Elam, the chairman of the athletics committee of the Board of Trustees. Although I did not officially apply for the job, I told him I would love to have it. I also talked very briefly with Coach Woodruff then.

When Bill Battle was selected about a week later, I went on about my business at Iowa State. I don't mean to sound egotistical about it, but I thought I was the man for the Tennessee job. There probably were a hundred coaches interested in it who

YOU CAN GO HOME AGAIN

also felt the same way. But I wasn't bitter; nobody owed me the job, and it was someone else's decision to make.

Somehow stories later made the rounds that the Majors family was sore at Woodruff, but, again, I had nothing to do with that. At that time I really didn't know Coach Woodruff well. I had bumped into him a few times at coaches' conventions and other professional or social events, but they only involved exchanging greetings. My dad knew Coach Woodruff quite well, however, and liked him.

I did not discuss the Tennessee position with the UT people during the five days that started with Bill Battle's resignation on Monday and ended with the Pitt–Penn State game on Friday night. At one point in midweek, however, Cas Myslinski told me that Coach Woodruff had called and had requested permission to talk with me after the Penn State game. After permission was granted, someone from Tennessee called me to set up a meeting for Saturday night, but for the life of me I cannot recall who made the call.

Tennessee ended its season at Vanderbilt on Saturday afternoon, and after that game Woodruff and my old teammate, Bill Johnson, who by this time was a member of the Board of Trustees at Tennessee, flew to Pittsburgh. I met with them on Saturday night. We talked for a long time and pretty well reached an agreement on salary and a budget for assistant coaches.

The next morning—Sunday—I flew to Knoxville with Woodruff and Johnson and met with the executive committee that makes all the major decisions regarding the school's athletic program. At that time it consisted of Dr. Ed Boling, the president; Dr. Jack Reese, the chancellor; Tom Elam, representing the Board of Trustees; Dr. Joe Johnson, the vice-president for administration; Dr. Earl Ramer, the faculty chairman of athletics; and Coach Woodruff, the athletic director. I was officially offered the job at that meeting, but I deferred a decision until I could talk with my family and the people at Pittsburgh.

Back at Pitt the following day, I met with Cas Myslinski, Chancellor Posvar, and other school officials; they all urged me to stay. It was pointed out, not unkindly, I think, that it often is very difficult for a coach to return to his old school. Ed Boznik, the assistant to the chancellor, gave me a copy of Thomas

My first staff as Head Coach, Iowa State, 1969 (*l* to *r*): Jack Blazek, Jackie Sherrill, Ollie Keller, Joe Madden, John Majors, Larry Lacewell, Jimmy Johnson, King Block, Gordon Smith.

My friend and mentor, Bob Dillon, of Des Moines, Iowa.

The Majors family honored at Neyland Stadium at half time of the 1971 Tennessee–Penn State game (*l* to *r*): Joe; Bob Majors; Mother; Daddy; Bill's sons, Bo and Mark; Shirley Ann Husband; John; Larry.

A favorite scene with Mary Elizabeth (age 3) and John Ireland (age 5).

Tony Dorsett's record-breaking run vs Navy, October 23, 1976.

Celebrating Pittsburgh's Sugar Bowl win on January 1, 1978, and undefeated national championship season.

Tony Dorsett and I at the Johnny Majors roast in Knoxville.

Visiting with Joe Paterno, for whom I have the highest respect as a person and a coach, 1974.

On the field with some loyal Pittsburgh rooters on Fans Day. *Front* (*l* to *r*): Jerry Ellis, Mary Elizabeth Majors, John Majors, Steven Massaro, David Massaro, Joey Massaro, John Ireland Majors. *Back* (*l* to *r*): Holly Ellis, Crissie Fulton, Peter Fulton.

On the sidelines with Daddy at the last game he coached, Sewanee vs Principia in 1977. This is one of my most prized photos.

With Daddy *(m)* and Bill *(r)* at a coaching clinic in July of 1965, my last extended time with Bill before his death in October.

Mother and Daddy with their grandchildren, 1977. *Front* (*l* to *r*): Andrew Tunnell, Ben Tunnell, Mary Elizabeth Majors, Inman Majors, Frank Majors, Tom Bill Husband, Bo Majors, Mark Majors. *Back* (*l* to *r*): John Ireland Majors, Jamie Copeland, Mother, Daddy, Elizabeth Husband, Kara Anne Copeland.

The bronze plaque presented in honor of Shirley Majors by his former players at Sewanee. It is displayed on the base of the flag pole at the football field on campus.

Speaking to UT fans at halftime of the Vols–University of North Carolina-Charolotte after being introduced as the new UT head football coach, December 1976 (*l* to *r*): Bob Woodruff, John Ireland Majors, Mary Elizabeth Majors, Mary Lynn Majors, Chancellor Jack Reese, John Majors.

A light moment on the field with Mary Lynn at Picture Day my first season at Tennessee.

Men with whom I had played or worked at Tennessee gathered on top of the press box as my luncheon guests, Spring 1978. *Front* (*l* to *r*): "Mr. Jim" Thompson, Gerald Hendricks, Mickey O'Brien, Harvey Robinson, Al Hust, Ralph Chancey, Jim Bradley, John Majors, Bob Woodruff. *Middle* (*l* to *r*): Dave Cantrell, Rev. Carson Frasier, Frank McCrosky, Pat Shires, Hal Bridges, Terry Sweeney, Ed Cantrell, Jim Smelcher, Bobby Scott, Cliff Williams, Bill Kincaid, Bobby Bringle. *Back* (*l* to *r*): Bill Anderson, Jed Winchester, Bo Shafer, Kyle "Buddy" Cruze, Tommy Hensley, Charlie Johnson, Bob Frye, Daddy Webb, Charlie Robinson, Frank Kolinsky.

The last of an "endangered species," Tennessee's single wing tailbacks, gathered in Knoxville in 1979 (*l* to *r*): Harold "Herky" Payne, Babe Woods, George "Bad News" Cafego, Walter Slater, Pat Shires, John "Drum" Majors.

Leading the Vols through the "T", 1978.

On the sidelines with offensive coordinator Bill Pace, 1981.

Mary Elizabeth dancing with Duffy Daugherty. Years earlier, he had told her, "I'd take you dancing if you didn't have to do your homework," to which she replied, "I just finished it." It took a while for Mary Elizabeth to collect on Duffy's promise!

The site of my hole-in-one at the Johnny Majors Invitational golf tournament, 1980 (*l* to *r*): Shirley Majors, Bill McCrary, Dr. Al Kuykendall, me, Jimmy Eanes, John "Skeeter" Bailey.

With Darrell Royal *(m)* and Murray Warmath *(r)* at the East Tennessee Football Hall of Fame dinner in which I presented the Robert R. Neyland Award to Coach Royal.

Visiting with Paul Montcastle from Nashville.

On the sidelines with Paul "Bear" Bryant prior to our nationally televised 1980 meeting in Knoxville. After the game, which Alabama won, 27–0, Coach Bryant told the interviewer, "When I came back out on the field at halftime and saw it pouring down rain, I sure felt bad for Johnny. I knew he'd have a tough time catching up."

Celebrating Tennessee's 1982 win over Alabama, our first since 1971.

There is nothing
that makes a priest
happier than the
smile of one of
his parishioners
face!
God Bless you
Jim +

The joy on my face shows following our 1982 victory over Alabama, my first after five defeats.

A much more dapper, relaxed coach arrives in Knoxville following the 1983 victory over Alabama, 41–34.

Running plays against the varsity defense in preparation for the 1983 Pittsburgh game.

An intense moment on the practice field. I enjoy on-the-field coaching during practice as much as anything I do.

My last pep talk to the Vols prior to our Sugar Bowl victory over Miami, January 1, 1986.

How sweet it was! Our victory at the Sugar Bowl was a fitting finish to an exciting, satisfying season in 1985.

With John Ireland and Mary Lynn at the Hula Bowl in Honolulu in January of 1986. I was honored to coach the East All-Stars team.

Our most recent family portrait.

Wolfe's *Look Homeward, Angel*, which contains that famous phrase, "You can't go home again." I was to hear that statement a lot, from a number of people, over the next few years. But I've never read the book.

Mary Lynn said, "This is a family affair, and we've got to have a family meeting about it." So she and I sat down with John and Mary, who at that time were twelve and ten. Everybody spoke his or her piece. Mary Lynn was not at all excited about going back to Tennessee. She was concerned that too much would be expected of me and that people would be unrealistic in light of the success we had enjoyed at Pittsburgh. John and Mary had reservations, too. Pittsburgh was their home, and the Panthers were their team. Tony Dorsett, Al Romano, and Matt Cavanaugh were their heroes. And, of course, moving would mean leaving their friends and school. Even after I decided to make the change, the thing that worried me the most was whether I had done the right thing as far as Mary Lynn and the children were concerned.

It was the most difficult decision I've ever had to make. Looked at from a practical point of view, it didn't make much sense for me to leave Pittsburgh. We had worked four hard years there and were coming off the greatest season anyone could have in college football. The future there was as bright as the present; the next year's team would be good enough to have a chance for another national championship. We loved Pittsburgh, our friends, the players, and the people at the university.

It is not easy to explain why I made the decision to return to Tennessee. It was not because I felt that Tennessee needed me more than Pittsburgh, or even that I loved my old school so much that I couldn't turn the job down. I did love Tennessee and still do, more now than ever. But I loved Pittsburgh, too. Basically, I think it was ego, a challenge, an "I'll show them" kind of thing. I wanted to prove something, and on looking back it seems downright silly to me today. I didn't have to prove anything, to me or to anyone else.

I never asked Pittsburgh for a counteroffer. I had decided right at the beginning that I would not turn the situation into a bargaining matter between the two schools. I felt I owed both of them more than that. I was aware that some of my friends and other Pitt supporters had gone to the chancellor and put together a financial package that far exceeded anything I had ever dreamed of making in coaching, and I am sure that if I had stayed at Pitt I would be a wealthy man today. But I told them I didn't even want to know what was in the package. I had not taken the Pitt job because of the money, and I didn't want to stay there for it either. I may have been foolish, but that is how I felt. As we get older, though, money and the security it brings begin to mean more to us; maybe I would take a peek at that proposition if I were faced with the same situation today. Who really knows?

It took me three or four days to reach the decision. My appointment as the head coach and assistant athletic director at the University of Tennessee was announced at a press conference at Stokely Center on the Tennessee campus on Saturday, December 4, 1976. Chancellor Jack Reese got a laugh when he introduced me by saying, "After an extensive nationwide search. . . ."

Mary Lynn and I were introduced to Vol fans at half time of Tennessee's basketball game with North Carolina–Charlotte. That's when I coined that phrase that's been quoted so many times since, "My blood runneth deep orange." I also said something else that went even straighter to the heart of the situation.

"I'm a hard worker, not a miracle worker."

I was aware of the emotional atmosphere surrounding my appointment. I had heard "When Johnny Comes Marching Home" on the radio, and I had been around football long enough to know that fans sometimes go to extremes, positive and negative. I wanted to be regarded as a football coach and, I hoped, a good one, not a magician. There was no way I was suddenly going to transform an ugly duckling into a beautiful swan.

◆·30·◆

Hard Times at Tennessee

My first close look at the Tennessee football establishment came in December of 1976. As I divided my time between Tennessee and Pittsburgh, I realized we had farther to go than I had thought when I took the job.

The facilities were rundown. The dormitory was in disrepair, with scroungy rooms and torn carpets on the floors. It looked bad and didn't smell much better, so one of my first priorities was to get Gibbs Hall refurbished. The stadium also needed some repairs, and Coach Woodruff and the administration were very cooperative.

I really didn't know the people with whom I would be working—Dr. Boling, Dr. Reese, and Coach Woodruff—so I did not know what it was going to be like working with them. I did have a couple of old friends in the athletic department in Gus Manning, the business manager, and Haywood Harris, the sports information director. Nobody anywhere is better than those two are at their jobs. They were tremendously helpful to me when I first came back to Tennessee, and they have been very supportive in all the ups and downs we've had. I also had known John Ward, the "Voice of the Vols," for a long time. John and I have worked together on our radio and television programs ever since I came to Tennessee. He is a thorough professional, one of the best in the business.

I found Bob Woodruff to be a genial man of great integrity. He and I have not agreed about everything that has come up, but the worst thing I can say about him is that he can be just as stubborn as I am. I discovered very early that he was not a man who was going to panic when things got tough. He never ran for cover. He and his delightful wife, Trudy, have been good friends to Mary Lynn and me.

Following a tough loss in one of the early years, Mary Lynn was standing outside the dressing room, apparently looking down in the dumps. Coach Woodruff came by and put his arm around her. "Honey," he said, "if you stay around long enough, there'll be some more days just as bad as this!"

The administration has given the football program unwavering support. At times I have wished we could move faster on some matters, especially on upgrading the facilities, but I realize that no coach gets everything he wants. We all have to answer to somebody, and I have had good, fair people to answer to at Tennessee.

Once my assistants and I got a close-up look at the squad, we knew that we had a long way to go. A successful football program starts with the players, and it soon was obvious that we did not have enough top quality athletes to compete at the top level of college football. I was frank about that when I answered questions from the press, and I was criticized by some as being too negative about our personnel. I knew that a lot of people had great expectations of me. Everywhere I went I would hear, "Hey, Coach, when are we going to beat Alabama?" and "When are we going to win the national championship?" I would have liked to be able to do those things immediately, too; but I wanted to make our situation as clear as I could.

The talent level at Tennessee in 1977 was somewhat higher than that at Iowa State when I went there in 1968. It was superior in numbers, but not in quality, to the squad I had inherited at Pittsburgh that had gone 1–10 the previous year.

The first time I met with the Tennessee players after the announcement had been made that I was to be their new coach, some of them showed up carrying snuff cups. Now I know a number of fine people who go around with a big chew of tobacco in their mouths, but I don't think our athletes should show up at a squad meeting dipping snuff. That rule went in right away.

I don't want to give the idea that they were problem children. Most of them were great kids, and I'll be grateful to them all my life for the effort they put into some of the toughest practice sessions I've ever coached. It started even before the spring practice, with our off-season conditioning. We instituted our "Fourth Quarter" drills in the "Bubble" across the street from Stokely Center. The weight and strength program was in dire need of upgrading. For the first few years, Tim Kerin had to double as both trainer and strength coach. Then we hired Bruno Pauletto to head up the weight and strength program; he has done an excellent job. That part of college football is much more important today than it was when I played. To stay competitive you must have your players on a productive off-season regimen.

Nothing is more important than the health of the players. Our athletes at Tennessee have been fortunate to have the very best in medical care from Dr. Bob Rubright, our team physician, and Dr. Bill Youmans, our orthopedic surgeon. These two men are not only outstanding professionals, but they are cooperative and friendly people as well.

Spring practice was mostly devoted to nuts and bolts things in 1978. Blocking. Tackling. Second effort. Pursuit. We taught the squads to get up off the ground and look for somebody else to hit. Players caught in a coaching transition pay a bigger price than those who come along after a program is established. They have to learn discipline, and selfishness has to be weeded out of their minds. Players have to be made to think in terms of "we" and "us" instead of "I" and "me."

Those young men worked long, hard hours, as did the coaches, but progress was painfully slow. At one session our offense was unable to move the ball at all. It was late in the day, but I got so exasperated I said, "Okay. Nobody leaves this field until we score." Forty-seven plays later somebody finally made it into the end zone.

I told Paul Davis about it in a telephone conversation the next day. "John," he laughed. "Those guys on defense must not have been too smart!"

I brought most of my Pittsburgh staff with me—Joe Madden as secondary coach and assistant head coach, Joe Avezzano as offensive coordinator and line coach, Bobby Roper as defensive coordinator and linebacker coach, Jim Dyar as defensive line coach, Bill Cox as quarterback coach, Henry Lee Parker as administrative assistant, and Tim Kerin as trainer. I also brought Bobby Jackson in from Vince Gibson's Louisville staff as running back coach and hired Bob Harrison from North Carolina State as receiver coach. From the old Tennessee staff I retained my old tailback coach, George Cafego, as kicking coach, along with Robbie Franklin as defensive end coach and Bill Higdon as recruiting coordinator.

Even though I knew we did not have a good football team, my heart was pounding as I ran through the big "T" for the first time as Tennessee's head football coach on opening day of the 1977 season. As hard as I was trying to concentrate on the game with California, I couldn't help but be aware of the emotional atmosphere. Joe Avezzano, who had been with me ever since the Iowa State days, told me later that when the Tennessee band played "When Johnny Comes Marching Home" it was one of the most moving things he has ever experienced in football.

"I couldn't help thinking of how many coaches had gone back home and had failed to make it," he said. "I was aware of the tremendous pressure you had to be feeling."

Mary Lynn had much the same thoughts. A few months earlier when I had made my "My blood runneth deep orange" talk at Stokely Center, I had ended up by saying that we all would have to buckle up our chin straps and get ready for rough times. "My Lord, what have we gotten ourselves into?" she said to herself.

But there I was, on the sidelines at Shields-Watkins Field, and I was there by my own choice. Whatever pressure there was— and I admit that I felt it—went with the territory. If there were some people who expected a quick fix, they were soon disappointed because California spoiled that first day for us, 27–17. Actually, we played a bit better than I had expected, and we were in the game until the fourth quarter when a fumbled punt took us out of it. We had had a hard time finding anybody to return punts and had to use a freshman, Junior Reid. He was from Humboldt, Tennessee, one of the first players I had recruited for Tennessee.

Junior felt terrible about it, but I told him he wasn't the first guy ever to fumble a punt and he wouldn't be the last. It was impossible not to remember my own experience in the 1957 Sugar Bowl game, and I had been a senior, not a freshman.

The red-shirt rule for freshmen came along soon after that, but it was a luxury we couldn't afford for a long time. We just didn't have enough good players at Tennessee to hold the good ones out during their first season. We have since reached that point, and our won-loss record reflects it. Almost invariably, when we have to play pure freshmen, I wish we hadn't done it once I look back on the situation. Yet sometimes just one great play can make it worth the risk. Where would Tennessee have been in the 1984 Alabama game without Andre Creamer's great punt return that set up the winning touchdown? There are exceptions to every rule.

There weren't many bright spots in either of our first two seasons. We went 4–7 in 1977 and 5–5–1 in 1978. I have never been prouder of a team than I was that 1977 team that went to Lexington and battled a great Kentucky team down to the wire before losing, 21–17. Kentucky was 10–1 that year, the best Wildcat team I've ever seen. But our boys took it to them. After the game I received a letter from an old Lynchburg friend, Bobby Harrison, that cheered me considerably. He quoted a passage from one of the sermons of my great-uncle, Tom Majors, an old fire-and-brimstone Methodist preacher: "It's better to be one foot from hell heading away from it than a hundred miles away heading toward it."

As far short as those first two teams were from the expectations of the Tennessee fans and the head football coach, they brought us a few painful miles along the way. No group of players I have ever coached meant more to me. It was fellows like Robert Shaw, Roland James, Brent Watson, Pert Jenkins, Dennis Wolfe, John Chavis, Jimmy Streater, and Scot Farrar who hung tough through some very trying times. They are as much a part of the success that Tennessee football has since experienced as those fortunate players who have been on teams with better records. The success all started with those two teams and with those long, hard days on the practice field.

I suppose that any football coach whose team is not doing well is aware that he is being criticized by some fans. I always try to stay apart from that as much as I can, not because I fear criticism but because most of it is only negative. Success in football, and in almost everything else, is the result of taking a positive approach. When people start telling me about what we're doing wrong, I tell them I don't want to hear it unless it's going to help us win.

Coaches usually are well insulated from the talk that you hear on the street corners, but our families aren't. Criticism can be much tougher on them than it is on us. My son John ran into a potentially awkward situation during those tough early years at Tennessee. He and a friend, Tim Burchett, were browsing through a downtown sporting goods store when they spotted a picture of me on the wall.

The clerk saw them looking at it. "We're going to get rid of that guy pretty soon if he doesn't beat Alabama," he said. "His days are numbered."

Naturally it made John mad, and his friend Tim was furious. Tim wanted to go after the guy right then, but John decided to handle it in a different way.

He hadn't planned to buy anything, but he picked up a couple of wristbands and told the clerk to charge them to his father's account.

"What's his name and address?" asked the clerk.

"Coach John Majors, University of Tennessee!"

We were a much better team in 1979. We won our first two games, against Boston College and Utah, which set up a big early season game with Auburn at Neyland Stadium. That day was memorable for several reasons.

That morning the athletics board had extended my contract for six more years. Then just before the game, a barrage of orange balloons was released at the stadium. What a sight! Then Gary Moore ran the opening kickoff back ninety-eight yards for a touchdown that put us on the way to a 35–17 victory. It was the first really big win we had at Tennessee, a least in terms of the impact on the public. Auburn had treated the Vols badly in the '70s, and by beating the Tigers we appeared to have climbed up a notch or two.

Tennessee had not beaten Alabama since 1970, but we threw a big scare into the Tide at Birmingham that season. We jumped out to a 17–0 lead in the first quarter against one of the great Alabama teams, and you never saw so much excitement on the sidelines. My phone to the press box was not working during our big push, and a couple of managers were scurrying around trying to find the trouble.

"Don't bother to fix it," I said. "We're doing pretty good without it!"

I still think we would have won that game if one play had worked in the second quarter. We were leading, 17–7, at the time; and Jimmy Streater found Anthony Hancock wide open with nothing between him and the goal line. The pass was a little long and the ball just skipped off Anthony's fingertips. Coach Bryant put Don Jacobs in at quarterback in the second half, and he ripped up our defense. They won the game, 27–17.

We went on to a 7–4 season and our first bowl game, the Bluebonnet. But we still were far shy of the consistency that we needed. For example, there were the back-to-back games with Rutgers and Notre Dame in November.

At the time Ben Byrd did a "Free Thought Association" prediction column every Saturday morning in the *Knoxville Journal*. It was a takeoff on people who take themselves too seriously at picking football winners. I've told him I blamed his famous, or infamous, "What are Rutgers?" piece for our 13–7 loss that day. Truthfully, however, I think most of the blame belonged to Coach Frank Burns and his fine team. I knew Rutgers was a good team and had tried to convince our players of it, but sometimes it is hard to get players to take a supposed underdog as seriously as they should.

The next week, however, we came back to overwhelm a good Notre Dame team, 40–18. It's always a big day for anybody to beat Notre Dame, and that win was a tonic for Tennessee football. We had not exactly been in the national spotlight for awhile. Hubert Simpson, who was rounding into a first class running back, scored four touchdowns that day.

In the Bluebonnet Bowl game we came from being down, 21–0, at half time to go ahead of Purdue, 22–21, in a fine comeback effort. We lost the game 27–22 when the Boilermakers made a late touchdown, but I was very encouraged about our outlook for the 1980 season. I figured it would be our best year yet, which just goes to show that nobody ever knows for sure what a football season holds in store.

Things started going badly before the season opened. I had to drop Hubert Simpson from the squad, and that hurt us a lot. He was our best running back, strong and fast, an outstanding talent, but he had been in trouble off and on since he first arrived in 1976 and had been dropped from school one year for disciplinary reasons. Hubert failed to show up for practice one Monday, and I felt I had no other choice than to drop him from the team. The staff and I called in the seniors and told them what had been done. When we asked for their opinions, only one disagreed with the decision.

The losses to Georgia and Southern Cal at Neyland Stadium in our first two games were among the toughest I've experienced. We had Georgia down, 15–0, early; but then a fumbled punt gave them a touchdown. Georgia brought Herschel Walker in off the bench; it was his first game, and I've often thought we did ourselves a disfavor by getting out to a big lead. The Georgia coaches told me they hadn't planned to use Herschel unless they were way ahead or way behind. Even after the Bulldogs went ahead in the fourth quarter, we still had a good chance to win the game. Then Glenn Ford fumbled on second down at the Georgia three-yard line with just two or three minutes left, and we lost it, 16–15. Georgia went on to a perfect season and the national championship.

The Southern California loss was even worse. The game was tied, 17–17, when their placekicker, Eric Hipp, hit a forty-seven-yarder as time ran out and the game ended.

Except for an absolutely flawless performance in a 42–0 win at Auburn and a couple of great offensive showings in late season victories over Kentucky and Vanderbilt, I would just as soon not remind myself of the 1980 season. At midseason, the worst rash of injuries we've ever had at Tennessee struck us; at one point we completely ran out of defensive ends. Injuries are a part of football and nobody wants to hear coaches cry about them, but they can tear a season all to pieces. I'm reminded of some of the wise words of Murray Warmath, one of the smartest men in the game, who coached some championship teams at Minnesota. "The football coach has two great enemies— injuries and the clock. He can't do anything about either one of them."

We hit a four-game tailspin in midseason, losing to Alabama,

Pittsburgh, and Virginia at home and to Ole Miss in that old jinx town, Jackson, Mississippi.

After the Ole Miss game I asked my dad for his impression of the game. Bless his honest heart, he didn't give me any jive. "It's not hardly worth talking about," he said.

·31·

Recruits and Rumors

My father died in April of 1981. He was doing one of the things he loved most—hunting—when he was stricken with a heart attack. Although he didn't live to see the happy days that were on the way in Tennessee football, he knew they were coming. A year and a half later, as I stood on the sidelines watching the clock tick down to the end of our first win over Alabama in eleven years, I found myself thinking, "I wish Daddy could be here."

He would have loved our 1981 team. It was his kind of team, one that went a long way on limited talent. After seeing what that team accomplished, I will never again be guilty of underestimating a group of young men. By traditional standards, 1981 was not a great season; we went 8–4, including a victory over Wisconsin in the Garden State Bowl. To my mind, however, it was the watershed season of my coaching career at Tennessee. To explain, I have to back up a bit in the story.

Those first four years had been the most agonizing period of my coaching career. Part of that was my fault; I made it hard on myself. By nature, I am a person who never sees a stranger. When I walk down the street, I greet most everyone I meet, but I was not that way in the early years after returning to Tennessee.

I was more reserved, more defensive, too much on guard. I knew that a lot was expected of me, and I had come to realize that the task of meeting those expectations was greater than I had thought when I had taken the job. If during that time I gave anyone the impression that John Majors was aloof, I sincerely regret it. I didn't mean to be that way, and I know that I'm not that way now. Since 1981 I think I have been more patient and less ornery. It's wonderful what good football players and an excellent staff can do for a head coach's personality!

Mary Lynn and I had made a lot of close friends wherever we had gone. They had been a source of great strength for us. We had been gone from Knoxville for seventeen years when we returned in 1977, and most of our old friends had long since moved to other places. Skeeter Bailey and his wife, Florence, still lived in Knoxville, thank goodness, and so did Ralph and Lennis Chancey. Bill Johnson and Bob Gleaves were two old teammates and buddies who lived reasonably close, in Sparta and Nashville respectively. And I established a good relationship with an older friend, Paul Mountcastle of Nashville. Paul is ninety-five years old as this is written, and the last time I saw him he was practicing his golf swing. He is one of the wisest men I know, as well as one of the kindest; and our hunting trips to his Blue Springs, Georgia, plantation have been high spots for us almost every winter.

Paul's plantation looks like a scene from the pre-Civil War South. The Woodruffs and Majors were admiring the view there one day when Trudy Woodruff turned to Mary Lynn. "Well, Scarlett, isn't it nice to be here?" she laughed.

Despite these old friends, and some others scattered here and there across the state, for a while we did not have the cluster of friends we had had in Ames and Pittsburgh; and we missed that tremendously. As time went on, though, our list of Knoxville friends grew and we felt more and more at home.

One of the most heartwarming things I've experienced in coaching happened after we had lost our first two games of the 1981 season in blowouts to Georgia and Southern Cal. At that time, public unrest with our program probably was at an all-time peak. A group of friends headed by Matthew McClellan took out a full page ad in the two Knoxville newspapers supporting us. The thing that touched me was not the effect it might have had on anybody's thinking—I doubt if it changed anyone's mind. It was just that our friends thought that much of us. We all need a little boost now and then, and that was a big one for me.

✦ ✦ ✦

In analyzing the hard times of those first four years, two key factors seem particularly important to me. The first was football players. You must have them to have good football teams, and we did not have enough. The second factor is recruiting, which, of course, is the answer to the first problem. Recruiting had become a tremendous challenge for Tennessee. The advent of the black player had changed the recruiting picture since I had been at Tennessee as an assistant coach. The states of Florida, Georgia, Alabama, and Louisiana now boasted most of the South's football talent. Obviously the Southeastern Conference schools in those states had a built-in advantage in recruiting.

It is up to us to overcome whatever recruiting disadvantages we have. Since those early years, we have had to get more than our share of the good players in Tennessee. Next we have had to get every athlete we could from the South, and then from every little pocket we could find in the eastern half of the country. To become competitive nationally, Tennessee has had to recruit on a national scale.

We came up with what was supposed to be a blue ribbon crop in 1978. Out of twenty-eight signees, ten were high school All-Americans, but you don't play football games with press clippings. Some of those recruits were overpublicized, some were overrated, and two of the genuinely outstanding players fell victim to illnesses that ended their careers before they got started.

Defensive tackle Lee Otis Burton, the most celebrated of the bunch, played only his freshman year. I'm convinced he would have been a great player. Twice during his one season with us I saw him run down fast-moving running backs from behind. And Tim Daniels, a fine-looking offensive guard, was a victim of cancer. Both of these young men recovered in time, thank the Lord; but neither of them could ever play football again.

Center Lee North, receiver Mike Miller, and some other fine players came out of that group. Only eleven of the twenty-eight made solid contributions to the team, though.

You cannot separate the coaching staff and recruiting; they go hand in hand. We underwent a drastic staff overhaul after the 1979 season. Joe Avezzano accepted the Oregon State head job and took Bobby Roper with him. Joe Madden went to the pros with the Detroit Lions. Jim Dyar left to go into private business; and Lynn Amedee, who had replaced Bill Cox as quarterback coach, left to take the head coaching job at the University of Tennessee at Martin.

I accept the reality of losing coaches, as I enjoy seeing my assistants move on to better things. I also understand professional ambition and frustration. Some of our coaches at that time were frustrated at not moving along faster.

Joe Madden, one of the best friends I'll ever have, was reaching the age when he felt he should be a head coach; and he was right. He was a quality person in every way. As much as I hated to lose him, I knew that it was frustrating for him to remain an assistant. I am happy that he has had the chance to go to pro ball and make the kind of money paid there.

I was also happy for Joe Avezzano, who also deserved a head coaching position. I had replaced Bobby Roper as defensive coordinator with Frank Emanuel the previous year, and Bobby's move was a natural one for him to make. Jim Dyar was a fine coach and as loyal an assistant as I've had and since leaving coaching he has enjoyed success in business in Knoxville.

I was lucky to be able to get my old friend, Bill Pace, to join me as assistant head coach and offensive coordinator. It was ideal timing for a man like Bill. Our offensive players were young and inexperienced, and we needed someone with Bill's stability and patience. Bill did a tremendous job in bringing our offense along, especially in 1981 when we lost our quarterback and had all inexperienced linemen. I also shifted Bobby Jackson to defensive coordinator and brought in two young coaches who have since become very important members of the best football staff in the country: Phil Fulmer, a former Vol player, for the offensive line; and Doug Mathews, who had been a great running back at Vanderbilt, of all places, to coach the offensive backs.

Those moves laid the foundation for the staff that was to come, but we suffered a one-year setback in recruiting. While only six of our 1980 signees ever made significant contributions, the 1981 group produced an even dozen contributors and the 1982 crop yielded eighteen. Thus we went from six to twelve to eighteen in successive years, and that was the cornerstone of the good years that came in the mid-'80s.

Among the signees in 1981 and 1982 were Alan Cockrell, Jimmy Colquitt, Fuad Reveiz, Johnnie Jones, Bill Mayo, Alvin

Toles, Jeff Smith, Charles Davis, Tim McGee, Joey Clinkscales, Terry Brown, Tommy Sims, and Tony Robinson. They each played central roles in our later success.

Bobby Jackson, who left us for the pros after the 1981 season, was one of the best recruiters I've ever known. An energetic little guy who stayed hot on the trail, he came up with some of our finest players. Lee Otis Burton, Willie Gault, Reggie White, Lee North, Bill Mayo, and Fuad Reveiz come to mind; and there were a lot more. Our current staff boasts good recruiters and, although I know that Tennessee always will have to fight to get football players, I feel very good about the situation now.

I went to Dalton, Georgia, with Bobby Jackson in December of 1980 to help him recruit Bill Mayo. Bill was the best offensive lineman coming out of high school in the South that season. We had a great visit with him and his charming mother. I was feeling very optimistic about our chances of recruiting Bill when he went into his room for a minute and came out carrying something.

"Do you like snakes?" he asked, holding one out for me to see.

I tried to show interest in the snake, and also the spiders he showed me later. I don't believe in misleading prospects, but in the case of Bill Mayo maybe I did stretch the truth a little bit. Nobody needed offensive linemen worse than Tennessee did at that time, and I probably would have handled a rattlesnake if it had taken that to get him to Tennessee. Bill turned out to be a jewel, an All-American guard and a solid team leader.

Another nagging worry pestered me in those first years at Tennessee. Somehow, somewhere, the rumor got started that I had been arrested on a number of occasions for drunk driving. The reports were totally untrue, but what could I do? Some people enjoy inventing and spreading lies, and I suppose it's only natural for other people to listen to them. Coach Woodruff eventually asked me if I would resent it if the athletic department checked into the matter.

"I would not only not resent it, I would welcome it," I said. "I've been trying to run these things down myself."

The check didn't turn up anything, but that didn't stop the rumors. They were everywhere, and the longer they spread the more embroidered they became. Then one day in March of 1982,

Ben Byrd and the editor of the *Knoxville Journal*, Ron McMahan, came to me with a suggestion.

"The rumors are all over the place, and we want to give you the chance to tell your side of the story," they said. "We think it will help clear the air."

I was reluctant to have the matter brought out in print. On the other hand, I wasn't happy about all the talk either. The situation was not going to improve unless something was done, so I agreed.

Ben's story, quoting me directly on the rumors that I had heard, ran across the top half of the first sports page in the *Journal*. It was then picked up by the Nashville and Chattanooga newspapers.

It turned out to be the best single thing that has happened to me since I came back to Tennessee. Since that day I have heard very few of these kinds of rumors, and the people at the papers tell me that the public reaction to the story was almost 100 percent positive.

That experience strengthened my faith in human nature. I have always felt that most people are naturally good and generous and that twenty people sometimes spoil things for twenty thousand. It only takes one person—like the twisted individual or individuals who sent the moving van to Bill Battle's house when he was disappointed in the Vols' performance—to give thousands of fans a bad name.

All these things—the recruiting battle, the staff changes, the rumors—combined to make those first four years back at Tennessee a hard grind, and I couldn't see any blue skies in the future.

Coming out of spring practice in 1981, I was more discouraged than at any time since I had returned to Tennessee. We had no experienced kickers, no proven quarterback, and a green offensive line. My report at the athletics council meeting was not very encouraging, and in the middle of my dirge, Joe Johnson interrupted me.

"Johnny, don't you have *anything* good to tell us?"

I know that a lot of Tennessee fans were restless in those times, and I don't blame them. I was too. About all I had going for me was an administration that stood behind me 100 percent.

I appreciated that. They are football fans, too, and they wanted to win as badly as I did. For their sakes, and mine, I am happy that I was a poor prophet.

Nineteen hundred eighty-one turned out to be a good year.

◆32◆

On and Off the Field

I don't want to imply that the life of a football coach is all seriousness or that we don't have a lot of fun. I have always had a well-rounded life, even though football is the most visible part of it. I like hunting, golf, travel, and a host of other things, and Mary Lynn and I have enjoyed a rich life together.

Mary Lynn and I have made a number of summer trips to England and Scotland, usually with Duffy Daugherty and his tour group. While there, I've played at the great golf courses, St. Andrews, Troon, Carnoustie, and others. On one day while I was golfing, Mary Lynn visited one of the old Scottish castles and spotted a distinguished-looking gentleman of about sixty, dressed in a kilt. It made such a natural picture that she asked him if he minded if she photographed him.

"No, not at all," he replied. "Where are you from?"

"The United States," she answered.

"Where in the United States?"

"Tennessee."

"Where in Tennessee?"

"Chattanooga."

"You mean where the train starts?"

Evidently the Chattanooga Choo Choo is world famous.

On another trip our party was trying to reach a destination in London, and I was wondering which subway train to take. I tried to get the information I needed from one of the station attendants.

I am often accused of talking too fast, and apparently I was in high gear that day. After a bit the gentleman stopped me. "Pardon me, sir," he asked. "What language are you speaking?"

One of my favorite events each year is the Johnny Majors Invitational golf tournament in late July or early August at the Tansi resort near Crossville, Tennessee. On the first day the football staff and other Tennessee athletic department people play host to the sportswriters and sportscasters who cover us on a regular basis. Then on the second day some of our leading boosters join us. Most of them are old friends, and I enjoy their company. It's also a last chance to get in a few rounds of golf before getting down to the serious business of the football season.

Ever since my dad introduced my brothers and me to golf when I was in high school, it has been a passion with me. I've played the game in many parts of the world, although I am only an average golfer. For a fleeting moment in 1980, though, I was a great player. I was playing in a sixsome, which included Skeeter Bailey; Dr. Al Kuykendall, a former Tennessee track star who now lives in Idaho; Bill McCrary, a big Vol booster; Jimmy Eanes of Nashville, my old sporting goods friend from Huntland days; my dad; and me.

The layout at Tansi has since changed, but then the ninth hole was a par three, 174-yard beauty. In this instance the first person to get a hole-in-one on the ninth hole would win a new car, a prize seldom claimed in golf tournaments for rather obvious reasons.

I hit a four-iron, saw the ball hit the front of the green, and then lost sight of it. Al Kuykendall started yelling, "Hole in one! Hole in one!"

Then the greens boy jumped in his golf cart and drove to meet us at the tee yelling, "Hole in one!" So we all started jumping up and down and yelling.

The boy, who looked to be about fifteen, said, "I'll have to have your name, please."

"John Majors," I answered.

"You're Johnny Majors?" he asked. And then *he* started jumping up and down!

My son John, who had just turned sixteen, had been bothering me for a new car to drive to school. I had told him a secondhand car was the best he could expect. One of his friends at Bearden High, John Cook, who later played tight end for Tennessee, heard about my winning the car on the news that night and told John about it. It didn't take him two minutes to get me on the phone. It was just the model he had wanted, a straight shift Chevelle.

"Okay," I said. "Okay, you can drive the car to school, but it's going to be my car, not yours. I don't believe in sixteen-year-old boys having new cars."

He growled about it for a while, but I knew he was delighted. So was I.

Struggling seasons take their toll on coaches and players alike, and we have to watch ourselves to make sure we don't go beyond the bounds of acceptable conduct on the practice field. During the 1975 season at Pittsburgh, I felt that all of us, me included, were losing our tempers too quickly and sometimes using language that we had no business using. So we set down a simple rule: No more of that.

In the early years at Tennessee, when so many things seemed to be going wrong, I backslid some on the language. I often use a megaphone with an amplifier on it when I'm on the coaching tower, and in the frustrations of bad practice sessions I slung two or three of them, smashing them beyond repair. Tim Kerin claims that I've destroyed five, but since I'm the head coach I'm going to insist it was only two or three.

Some of my other coaches started letting things get to them, too, so at a staff meeting I told them it was time for us to reactivate the old rule: No more cussing or throwing things.

"Lord knows I'm not preaching any sermons to you. I'm more guilty than anybody," I said.

It wasn't long after that two more megaphones were destroyed accidentally. One of them was stepped on inadvertently, and I took the other down to the field with me and left it on the ground, where a cherry picker, which we use to lift photographic equipment ran over it. Guess who was driving it!

Two more megaphones down the tube, and I hadn't even raised my voice! I took a lot of kidding from the other coaches, who insisted that I must have smashed them myself.

Like most coaches, I can get pretty preoccupied during the week leading up to a big game. Phil Fulmer and some of the other coaches on the Tennessee staff decided to pull a stunt one day, but in my preoccupation with the upcoming game I was oblivious to what happened. I was in the film room with the offensive staff, checking out our upcoming opponent, and didn't realize that a practical joke had been planned for Kippy Brown.

Kippy, our receiver coach, is a notorious cigarette moocher who never carries his own pack. I quit smoking several years ago, but on rare occasions I'll light one up without really thinking what I am doing. A pack of cigarettes was sitting on the table in the film room that day and, without thinking, I reached out and took one.

Actually the pack had been put there for Kippy's benefit. Phil Fulmer and some of the other coaches had "loaded" some of the cigarettes with little explosive charges. I had to be told about what happened later, because I was oblivious to the whole thing. Phil says the whole staff almost fell on the floor in silent prayer that I hadn't gotten one of the loaded ones.

But I had. After I took a couple of puffs, it popped. After a couple more, it popped again. After two or three more explosions, I mashed it out in an ashtray and commented, "This must be an awfully old cigarette."

I guess I was concentrating on the films so much that I was oblivious of what was happening around me.

Life has its humorous moments, and the life of a coach has more than its share. I find some of the richest times come as surprises, both on and off the field.

·33·

On the Upswing

Every time the University of Southern California scores, a warrior on a horse gallops around their field. I've often wondered why that horse didn't die of exhaustion after our 43–7 loss to the Trojans at the Los Angeles Coliseum in the second game of the 1981 season. Following a 44–0 loss at Georgia the previous week, as we rode the plane back to Knoxville, I found myself wondering where our victories, if any, were going to come.

There was no premonition of the future, yet before the season was finished, we would get eight wins. The entire season was a testimonial to a gutsy bunch of players who didn't know they were supposed to be a mediocre team. They won their games every which way, hanging on by their teeth for a victory one Saturday, kicking a game-winning, last-second field goal the next, losing key players, and coming up with heroic replacements off the bench.

We lost freshman quarterback Alan Cockrell, who had made a sensational first start in a 42–0 win over Colorado State, in the first series against Auburn at Neyland Stadium. Steve Alatorre took Alan's place, and we hung on for a 10–7 win, with Bill Bates having a tremendous game. Then we won over Georgia Tech the following Saturday by the same score, 10–7. It was a storybook win over Wichita State, 24–21, when freshman Fuad Reveiz kicked a twenty-eight-yard field goal as time ran out. The stars were in the right places for us that season.

Tennessee has been blessed with great placekickers—Alan

Duncan, Fuad Reveiz, and Carlos Reveiz. All were superb in the clutch, as well as having strong, accurate legs. Fuad came to us almost as a gift out of the blue. We came out of spring practice in 1981 without an established kicker, and I told the staff to keep their eyes open for one. Bobby Jackson came up with Fuad, who had been a linebacker in high school in Miami and had only kicked a few field goals. The report, however, was that he had a big league leg. Fuad had already signed with a junior college out West, and it was well into the summer before we found out about him. He and his parents came to Knoxville for a visit, and I sat talking with them in Neyland Stadium while some of our other kickers were practicing on their own.

"I can kick better than those guys," Fuad said.

"If I wanted a scholarship, I'd say the same thing," I answered.

Mrs. Reveiz spoke up. "You don't know Fuad. He means what he says, and he can do it."

I didn't know if he could kick a lick, but sometimes it pays to play hunches. This young man and his parents were class people all the way, and I made a quick decision. "You've got a scholarship," I said and held out my hand.

I haven't counted the number of games Fuad won for us over the next four years, but it was a lot. If you add what his younger brother, Carlos, did for us in the 1985 championship season, signing Fuad Reveiz was about the best impulse action I ever took.

After the 1981 season, I felt that we were finally ready to get in the ring with the heavyweights. We still didn't have as many big linemen as we needed, and we weren't as deep as some other teams, but we had some fine skill players on offense, including the most electrifying receiver-kick returner in the nation in Willie Gault. I never had had a player who could run a 4.2 forty before Willie. He was a great athlete and a fine person, and he developed the skills he needed to match his natural talent. I knew that if we could get the ball to Willie often enough, we would put a lot of points on the board.

The key to the team's future was the physical condition of Alan Cockrell. Alan, from Joplin, Missouri, was the best quarterback we had signed at Tennessee and one of the four best I had ever seen in looking at hundreds of high school prospects on film over the years. The others were Matt Cavanaugh, Art Schlicter, and Tony Robinson. We had just signed Tony out of Tallahassee, Florida, that spring.

Alan's knee injury the previous year was one of the worst I've seen, and Tim Kerin and our orthopedic surgeon, Dr. Bill Youmans, both had reservations about his future. Nevertheless Alan is a great competitor who paid an awesome price to rehabilitate his knee and get back on the football field. The knee held up through the next two seasons, and he helped put Tennessee on the road back to football prosperity.

The highlight of the 1982 season, and still the single biggest game that Tennessee has won in my time as coach, was that October day at Neyland Stadium when we finally ended Alabama's domination after eleven games. Old Shields-Watkins Field has seen a lot of great moments, but very few have matched that one. It is extremely difficult to break the ice against a team that has lorded it over you for a long time. The winners are used to winning and the losers to losing and, no matter how determined or how confident the players seem to be, there always will be that little seed of uncertainty running around somewhere in the back of the mind.

Our 35–28 win that day got Tennessee started on a four-game streak of our own over Alabama. I doubt if there ever have been four more tense, exciting games played in successive years between two old rivals. We ended up with four wins, but they could just as easily have been four losses. In 1982 Mike Terry intercepted a pass in the end zone in the last few seconds to preserve the win. In 1983 we won, 41–34, when Johnnie Jones sprinted sixty-six yards in the fourth quarter to break the tie. We came from fourteen points down in the last seven minutes to win, 29–28, in 1984, with Tony Robinson scoring the winning points on an option run for a two-point conversion. And in 1985 a great defensive play by Dale Jones stopped Alabama, and we held on to win, 16–14.

Bear Bryant coached against Tennessee for the last time in 1982. He died in January of the following year. It was also the first time I had coached a team that beat one of his teams; so the victory had a double special meaning. He was very gracious after the game.

"Johnny, you had a great game plan," he said.

I appreciated his kind words, but I didn't really agree with them. The game plan was okay, but mainly what we had were players like Alan Cockrell, who passed for almost 200 yards; Willie Gault, who caught a long touchdown pass and set South-eastern Conference career punt and kickoff return records; Chuck Coleman, who rushed for 139 yards; and a defense that pretty well shut down the nation's number two team until mid-way in the fourth quarter.

It was as wild a crowd as I've ever seen. Tennessee fans refused to leave, even after they tore down the goal posts. I had finished meeting with the squad and was headed for the press interview when Gus Manning stopped me.

"John, they're still out there," he said.

I sent some of the players back onto the field to take another bow, and when I walked out of the locker room almost an hour after the game had ended, there still were several hundred fans milling around the field.

Coach Bryant had always been extra nice to me when I was a young coach. Whenever I'd see him at coaches' conventions, he usually was with Coach John McKay of Southern Cal; when he would notice me, he would invite me to join them. I was much too awed at the time to take him up on his invitation very often, but in more recent times I had spent some time with him on occasion.

The first year I was back at Tennessee, I even invited myself to watch an Alabama practice one day. I was in Tuscaloosa on a Monday to give a talk, and we had an open date coming up the next Saturday. That meant we wouldn't practice that Monday, so I called Coach Bryant at his office.

"Coach, this is John Majors," I said. "I've always wanted to observe one of your practice sessions. Since I'm in town today and we've already played you, I thought maybe this would be a good chance."

It was pretty clear that he wasn't crazy about the idea.

"Oh, Johnny, you don't want to do that," he said. "You're not going to learn anything from us. We're not going to do anything much today, anyway."

I wasn't going to let him off the hook that easily. I knew that he had picked General Neyland's brains when he was a young coach, and I was going to try to cash in that little voucher. So I kept after him.

"Oh, well, you can come on, but you're not going to learn anything," he sighed.

When I got there, he was a perfect host. He took me up on his tower and spent a long time talking about General Neyland, Bowden Wyatt, and the Tennessee–Alabama rivalry. His assistants later told me that he had limited them on what they could use while I was there.

The Saturday following that first big win over Alabama was a day that will live in infamy as far as I am concerned. When the team reported back to the practice field on Monday, I had a gimmick rigged up for them, a little makeshift platform covered with blankets and a sheet.

"This is Cloud Nine," I said. "Each one of you is going to jump off it, and then we will be down off Cloud Nine and we'll start getting ready to play Georgia Tech."

I still don't think it was a bad idea, but the bottom line is that it didn't work. Tech, which didn't have a good year at all, beat us like a rug. One of the toughest things for a football team to learn is how to handle a big victory. No matter how hard you preach against it, there always is the danger of euphoria sneaking in. I know it happens, as I have experienced it myself, but not since that Tech game in 1982.

We finished the regular season 6–4–1 and then lost to Iowa, 28–22, in the Peach Bowl in Atlanta. We had scored a lot of points that season, but so had our opposition. It was clear to me that we had to do something to make our defense more competitive.

When Bobby Jackson left after the season was over to join the Atlanta Falcons' coaching staff, I made a pitch to lure my former colleague, Ken Donahue, back to his alma mater. Ken had been Alabama's defensive coordinator for twenty years, but since the Bear was gone I thought he might be interested. He was, and we almost got him that time. However, he decided to stay on at Alabama, and I hired Larry Marmie from the North Carolina staff. Larry got our people playing sound defense in 1983. We also brought in a new offensive coordinator, Walt

Harris, from Illinois, to replace Al Saunders. Al, who had been with us for one year, took a job with the San Diego Chargers.

The 1983 season turned out to be our best yet. With a good bounce of the ball here and there, it could have been a great one. We lost two early games to Pittsburgh and a very strong Auburn team. We hadn't beaten a strong team when we went into the Louisiana State game at Neyland Stadium in early October. Some newspaper stories that week implied that Tennessee was never going to win big under Majors; but we beat LSU, 26–0, went down to Birmingham the next Saturday and beat Alabama, 41–34, and winding up 9–3, including a well-played win over Maryland in the Florida Citrus Bowl. The highlight was the second straight win over Alabama in another barnburner.

I know that Gene McEver's run in 1928 and Johnny Butler's run in 1939 were every bit as good as legend has them, but I think Johnnie Jones' run for the game-winning touchdown stacks up with them. I can see that play right now in my mind— Cockrell moving down the line to the left on a counter option, pitching back to Jones, and Johnnie bursting through the hole. What a lot of fans didn't realize was that we had three wide receivers on the field on that play, and all of them made downfield blocks to help clear the way for Johnnie. General Neyland and Bowden Wyatt would have been proud to see the execution on that play.

We played good, sound defense in '83. We had one big play defensive man in Reggie White, the best defensive lineman I've ever coached. He could absolutely dominate an entire side of the line of scrimmage. We had looked for him to play like that in his first three seasons, but he had been merely good then. In his senior year, though, he was great. He was a good person, too, a very religious youngster who already was an ordained minister.

But Reggie was not above conning a person a little if he could get away with it. Willie Gault and he used to take it upon themselves to come to me with team problems, and I sometimes suspected that they had appointed themselves team spokesmen.

Back in 1981 we almost blew the game with Vanderbilt by not playing any defense. So we went back to the basics on the practice field as we prepared for the Garden State Bowl game. After two or three days of that, Reggie and Willie showed up in my office.

"Coach, we thought that a bowl game was supposed to be a reward," said Reggie. "This is like spring practice. The players are unhappy."

"People who play like we did against Vanderbilt don't deserve a reward," I answered. "I'll tell you what. If you beat Wisconsin, we might take you over to New York for a big meal in a nice restaurant. That can be your reward."

The team performed like I hoped it would, and we won an exciting victory over Wisconsin, 28–21.

The 1984 season was notable for the appearance of the greatest quarterback talent I've ever had the pleasure of coaching. From the day he arrived on campus, Tony Robinson amazed all of us with his touch on the long throws. Sixty-five yards for him was like thirty for most other passers. He had long, tapering fingers; and he held the ball with his right forefinger at the end, much like Terry Bradshaw. Tony had been with us for two years, but he had not really worked hard enough at the detail part of his position—the signal calling, and reading and checking—but Walt Harris gave him an education that season. Walt has a fine football mind, and I doubt that any coach has ever worked harder with a quarterback than he did with Tony. The result was one of the most exciting football players in Tennessee history.

Robinson's great play, along with the pass catching of Tim McGee and the running of Johnnie Jones, gave us an outstanding offense. Tony led us from two touchdowns behind to an unbelieveable win over Alabama to keep that streak going. He had some other great performances, too; but without Reggie White, our defense just wasn't strong enough for us to be a contender for the conference championship. We were too soft, had very few takeovers or big plays, and finished way down the list in Southeastern Conference defensive statistics. Our 7–4–1 record, including a tough 28–27 loss to Maryland in the Sun Bowl, could have been a lot better if we could have put some pressure on the opponents' offense.

We needed to be tougher, more aggressive and physical on defense. While I was wondering where to find a coach who could teach those things, a telephone call from Tuscaloosa provided the answer. It was my old friend Ken Donahue.

·34·

Color it Orange

I would like to be able to say that I was smart enough to know that 1985 was going to be *the* year before the season started. The fact is that coming out of spring practice, I was very uneasy about the defense and the kicking game.

When you talk about defense and kicking to an old Tennessee football man, you've said it all. The game changes its look every now and then, but one eternal truth still prevails: the offense scores points, but defense and kicking win games. I knew we were going to have to depend on two untried kickers, punter Bob Garmon and placekicker Carlos Reveiz, Fuad's younger brother. On defense, we had very little experience in the line and at the linebacker positions, but I was very pleased with the attitude and effort of all the players. It was the most pleasant spring practice we had held at Tennessee.

We had added leadership and expertise to our staff that money couldn't buy in hiring Ken Donahue. Alabama had planned to move Ken into an administrative job, but he wasn't ready to leave the field yet. When he called, I quickly offered him the job of defensive line coach, and when Larry Marmie left to take a job at Arizona State, Ken was the automatic choice for defensive coordinator.

Ken is still the same old Donahue I had worked with more than twenty years earlier, a really unique individual, totally dedicated to football and totally honest. His long working days are famous in the coaching profession. I am reminded of that old story about the time when Bear Bryant, leaving for home after a long day, was stopped by a man outside the Alabama fieldhouse.

"Coach, you left the light on in your office," he said.

"No, that's just Donahue up there making a legend out of me," answered Bryant.

The addition of Donahue completed a coaching staff that I wouldn't trade for any in college football: Donahue, Mel Foels, Ron Zook, and Dick Bumpas on defense; and Walt Harris, Phil Fulmer, Doug Mathews, Kippy Brown, and David Cutcliffe on offense. I never once had to crank up anybody during the '85 season; each of these men is highly motivated and highly competitive. They make things a lot easier for their head coach.

I could say much the same thing about the 1985 squad. I don't think I had to call a single player into my office for disciplinary reasons all season. Every coach knows how important that is; the good teams almost always are the ones with the least dissension.

I had no fears about our offense. With Tony Robinson, the best receiver in the country in Tim McGee, some good young running backs, and a veteran offensive line, we figured we would have one of the most explosive teams in the country.

The opening game with UCLA on ABC-TV at Neyland Stadium confirmed my early impressions. With Robinson having a great day, the offense took charge of the game in the second and third quarters; and we went into the last six minutes leading by sixteen points. That 26–26 tie was a big disappointment, especially after we apparently had the game under control. I know some fans thought we had gotten too conservative, and I felt that maybe we lost some of our aggressiveness and got too oozy on defense.

Sometimes just one play can swing a football game. In studying the films, I saw where we came within an inch or two of breaking it wide open in the fourth quarter. UCLA had to score two touchdowns and two two-point conversions to tie us, and we had them backed up inside their own ten on third down and ten. They hit a forty-four-yard pass that touched off their first drive, but the films showed that Chris White missed an interception by a fingernail. Chris led the nation in interceptions in 1985, and I'm convinced that a little later in the season he would have grabbed that pass.

After the game I told the press I was disappointed but not discouraged. In fact, I was encouraged by the way the defense had played throughout most of the game.

The Auburn game the following Saturday was the one that got me to thinking that this Tennessee team might be a team of destiny. We were on ABC for the second straight week, and we jumped into the national spotlight by beating the number one-ranked team with as fine a performance as any coach could want. We were ahead, 24–0, at half, and the 38–20 final score didn't really reflect the difference in the two teams on that particular day.

Our defense got a little soft again at the end of the game, but it did a great job on Bo Jackson throughout most of the afternoon. Any time someone like him is held to eighty yards, a defense has done a day's work. Robinson's great play got him on the cover of *Sports Illustrated* and won him AP and UPI Back of the Week honors. All in all, it was a great day for Tennessee.

Going into the game, I had felt that we had a good chance to win. Auburn had switched from the wishbone to the I formation, and it always takes a few games to get a new offense in rhythm. The most satisfying thing for me, however, was the way our people lined up jaw to jaw with Auburn in the line. The Tigers had a well-deserved reputation as hard noses. All Pat Dye-coached teams have that personality.

The Southeastern Conference always has been a league of trench warfare, as opposed to the wide-open style of play seen in some other parts of the country. To compete in the conference, a team has to hold up its end of the stick in the physical part of the game. In my early years at Tennessee, we had lost several games because we were not big or strong enough to compete. When our players matched up with the Southeastern Conference's resident hard noses at their own game, I knew that we had leaped a big hurdle.

We were 2–0–1 going into the game with Florida at Gainesville on October 12, after a narrow escape with Wake Forest, 31–29. Wake Forest never should have played us that close, but once again the defense got too soft in the fourth quarter.

Even though we lost to Florida, 17–10, I came away feeling better about the overall picture than I had in the earlier games. For the first time the defense played well for the full game. Kicking actually decided the Florida game. Florida made some great punts and backed us into a corner to get strong field position for a couple of third quarter touchdowns. There had been a lot of pregame ballyhoo over Tennessee's vote to deny the Gators the 1984 Southeastern Conference championship because of recruiting violations, but the Florida crowd couldn't have been more sportsmanlike. Florida was a complete team with no major weaknesses, the best team we played all season.

I don't know if any other team in the country faced the kind of schedule we did in the first half of 1985. Five of the first six opponents were top twenty teams, four of them in the top ten at one time or other. We never had that feeling that if we could get by this Saturday we would get some relief the next one. We kept leaping back and forth between the frying pan and the fire. After that tough loss to Florida, the next stop was Birmingham, the best Alabama team since Ray Perkins had replaced Bear Bryant.

The Alabama series means so much to me. The first three Tennessee games I ever saw were against Alabama. So much of Southern football history has been written in the Tennessee–Alabama series. Also, beating Alabama means so much to Tennessee fans.

In the summer of 1982 Mary Lynn and I had guests from Pittsburgh in town for the Knoxville World's Fair. We took them to the fair and dropped in at the Strohaus, where a band was playing some great German music. When we came in, the band interrupted a polka and started playing "Rocky Top."

Somebody yelled, "When are we going to beat Alabama, Johnny?"

There was a spontaneous cheer from the audience. Somebody started chanting, "Alabama, Alabama," and before long the whole crowd was on its feet roaring. "ALABAMA! ALABAMA! ALABAMA!"

Our friends were amazed and said, "John, if I were you, I believe I'd get around to beating Alabama soon!"

That's how strong the Tennessee-Alabama rivalry is.

Until Tony Robinson went down early in the fourth quarter of the 1985 game, it looked as if we might be headed to a hard-earned, but clearcut, victory. We were ahead, 13–7, and had moved inside the Alabama ten.

The play was a bootleg pass, and Tony scrambled when he couldn't find a receiver. Tony was a hungry player, always scratching for that extra yard, and he waited just an instant too long before hitting the deck. Two of Alabama's great defensive men, linebacker Cornelius Bennett and nose guard Curt Jarvis, hit him as he was going down. Some of the Tennessee fans thought they gave Tony a cheap shot, but that's not really true. They were clean hits. The Tennessee–Alabama rivalry has been a fierce one, but you almost never see the players on either side taking cheap shots or shooting off their mouths at each other. This was the same kind of game.

I could tell Tony was hurt badly from the look on Tim Kerin's face when he came off the field. Four times during our years together Tim has had to tell me that we had lost our quarterback to a serious leg injury. First it had been Matt Cavanaugh and Robert Haygood, then Alan Cockrell; now it was Tony Robinson. If I were like that old Greek king who used to kill the messengers who brought bad news, Tim would have been dead a long time ago.

"It's bad, Coach," he said. "I'm afraid Tony's through for the year."

In moments like that a football coach has no time to stand around feeling sorry for himself. The most talented quarterback I had ever coached had played his last down for Tennessee, but the game had to be played. I got on the phone to the press box and talked to Ken Donahue.

"Tony's out," I said. "I just wanted you to know so you can make your defensive plans. Your people are going to have to suck it up and hold them off, but don't say anything to Walt Harris just yet."

I didn't want to bother Walt while he was concentrating on the situation on the field. We were in four-down territory, and we needed to put something on the board to move out of one-touchdown range. We wanted to make it as hard as we could for Alabama to come from behind to win.

As soon as Carlos Reveiz kicked a field goal to stretch the lead out for us, I called Walt. "Keep your chin up," I said. "Tony won't be back in this ball game, and probably not the rest of the season. We're going to have to put that out of our minds right now and concentrate on winning this game."

What happened during the rest of the game was one of those rewarding experiences that make coaching so meaningful. Alabama made it tougher on us by driving for a touchdown on the next possession, and we had to face about ten of the longest minutes I've ever lived through as a coach. We weren't able to move the ball ourselves, but I blamed that on the situation rather than on Daryl Dickey. There is nothing in football any more difficult than for a backup quarterback to come off the bench ice cold in a big game.

On his first pass, Daryl made the only bad throw I saw him make all season. One of Alabama's outside linebackers had the ball in his hands and could have run it back a long distance, but he dropped it. Sometimes we tend to dwell on our bad luck and overlook the good. Losing Tony Robinson was a cruel blow, but the football gods were smiling down on us when that ball struck the ground.

Our defense grew up that afternoon. Three times we held off Alabama drives, once on a tremendous defensive play. Dale Jones, our great outside linebacker, rushed quarterback Mike Shula, blocked the pass from not more than a yard away, and then caught the ball before it hit the ground! That saved the day for us.

I have never seen a more courageous victory by a football team.

Daryl Dickey moved up to the number one quarterback spot for the next game, which was with Georgia Tech. The 6–6 tie gave a lot of people the wrong slant on Daryl. Some fans think that you can throw a football game wide open any time you choose, but it doesn't work that way. Sometimes you get caught up in a game where the two defenses just won't give up anything; then you wind up in an old-fashioned kicking duel and battle for field position.

That's what happened in the Georgia Tech game. Tech had one of the strongest defenses we had to face all year. Admittedly, we were a little more conservative than we would have been if it had not been Daryl's first game. A lot of people left early in the fourth quarter and missed an exciting finish. Daryl did a great job of rushing us downfield with the hurry-up offense, and Carlos Reveiz popped a fifty-one-yard field goal as time ran out, giving us a tie. Ties are like people; no two are ever exactly the same. I didn't like the one in the UCLA game, but I was happy for this one.

Daryl Dickey went on from that game to lead us to the Southeastern Conference championship and a smashing Sugar Bowl victory. I have never been happier for a football player. He had had more reason than most to be discouraged. He was an excellent football player, but he had five years of hard work and very little playing. Nevertheless, he hung tough, assisted the younger quarterbacks, helped along the sidelines during the games, and was prepared when the time came.

Daryl set a school record for the most consecutive passes thrown without an interception, won the Most Valuable Player award at the Sugar Bowl, and wound up an unselfish career as a campus hero. He also set a new record for pass completion percentage and never lost a game as a starting quarterback. His background as a coach's son helped him immeasurably, of course.

Coach Dickey reserved his judgment until after he had seen Daryl turn in a cool job against a salty Memphis State defense at Memphis. When that game was over, he turned to his wife, Joan, and said, "We're on the way to the Sugar Bowl."

I wish he had let me know. We were, more or less, in a tie with Alabama and LSU, who were playing that same afternoon at Baton Rouge. The only thing that would really help us would be for neither team to win, and I had brought that up at my press conference in Knoxville earlier in the week.

"I'm predicting a tie," I said, but that was more wishful thinking than it was prophecy.

I have a rule that the team bus always runs on time, but we held it up for a few minutes at Memphis while we followed the finish of the LSU–Alabama game on radio. The score was tied when LSU stormed downfield at the end to set up a short field goal. Gus Manning turned to me and said, "Well, it looks like LSU's going to pull it off."

"No, he's going to miss it," I said. "This is our year."

"I'll bet you a dollar he makes it," laughed Gus.

I never bet on football games, but I already had a lot riding on this one.

"You got it," I said.

The LSU kicker missed, and Tennessee turned out to be the only winner in that game. I'll never spend Gus's dollar. I have it framed, and it sits on my desk right now, along with another little memento of the 1985 season. After we beat Kentucky at Lexington with some sensational Dickey-to-McGee passes in the second half, Bob Woodruff came to the dressing room and gave me a little pack of sugar with a picture of a wildcat on it.

Sixteen years of pent-up emotion erupted when we beat Vanderbilt in the final game of the season at Neyland Stadium. Not a soul left the stadium until the goal posts were torn down and the Sugar Bowl invitation had been officially extended and accepted.

I was happy for our players, our coaches, our school, myself, and the Tennessee fans, the best in college football.

·35·

So Many Happy People!

I have never experienced anything quite like the Sugar Bowl of January 1, 1986. I'm not just talking about the game, although I'll never forget it.

It was all those thousands of Tennessee people who took over New Orleans in the last week of December. They made this such a special week for our team, and for Mary Lynn and me. It was like a Tennessee festival, a homecoming. Everywhere I looked, every street I walked down, there were those great Big Orange fans—friendly, happy Tennessee supporters. Our greatest pleasure was just walking along the streets, sometimes down to the French Quarter, and visiting with people from Tennessee. From every part of the state—Bristol, Oneida, Waynesboro, Nashville, Knoxville, Memphis, Chattanooga, and those two garden spots of the universe, Huntland and Lynchburg—they came. It was wonderful to meet them and to talk football.

They were happy, friendly folks. Mary Lynn and I would stop and talk with as many of them as we could, signing autographs and passing the time. Sometimes bowl crowds get a little out of hand, but wherever I went in New Orleans people talked about how well-behaved the Tennessee fans were. I got the feeling that they were just happy to be there and that even if the game went the wrong way, it wouldn't spoil things for them.

I told Mary Lynn, "I think our fans are so excited that unless we get bombed, they're going to go back home feeling it's been a great year."

I have no idea how they got their hands on all those tickets.

The school's supply ran out early, but the fans latched on to them somehow. Some of them even got tickets from Miami. My son John shared an apartment in Knoxville with his friend Greg Gundlach, another pole vaulter on the Tennessee track team. Their phone was listed under the name of John Majors, and it rang incessantly with calls from people wanting tickets. Finally John put a recording on the automatic answering device, "Greg and John aren't in right now. If you want Sugar Bowl tickets, you should call the football office." And then the rascal gave them my office number!

I don't know how many Tennessee fans were in New Orleans—I've heard estimates of fifty thousand—but on the afternoon of the game, Mary Lynn and I stood at the window of our room in the Hyatt Regency and watched a seemingly endless stream of people dressed in orange making their way to the Superdome.

Mary Lynn's reaction? "It looks like an invasion. Like an orange army."

I agreed.

At the time I had no idea that we were perched on the edge of such a monumental victory. I had too much respect for the Miami team for that. My old friend and former assistant, Jimmy Johnson, had a team with no apparent weaknesses, and a lot of people figured that the Hurricanes were the best team in the nation. Penn State, ranked number one, was to play Oklahoma in the Cotton Bowl, and Jimmy put in a couple of plugs for the national championship in case Miami beat us and Oklahoma beat Penn State. He was second-guessed some for that later, but I might have done the same thing if I had been in his place. If his team had won the game, he would have had a reasonable claim because Miami had beaten Oklahoma early in the season. I don't think he overlooked Tennessee at all.

The team had traveled to New Orleans the day after Christmas, and our practices had been good ones. I had given the squad a lot of free time in which to see the sights. That's been my practice for all bowl games, and it is based on my experience as a Tennessee player. When our 1956 team went to the Sugar Bowl, we stayed in a hotel on the outskirts of New Orleans. We had had nothing to do except practice, see an occasional movie, bowl, and look at each other.

That was the only thing I felt the Tennessee staff did wrong. So early in my coaching career I vowed that if I ever took a team to a bowl game, the players would get to live it up a little.

Since it is the players who get a team to a bowl game, I feel they deserve the opportunity to see the sights and have a good time. They are responsible young men, and they should be treated like adults. At the same time, at Tennessee we make it plain to them that they must measure up to their responsibilities and abide by the rules we make. If they don't, there will be a plane ticket home for them before the game is ever played. That certainly does not mean that any part of the game preparation is overlooked. I have taken teams to eleven bowls in eighteen seasons as a head coach, and I have treated every team the same way. Every team has made me proud of them, even those that did not win, because they worked hard, never gave up, and became a tremendous credit to their families, their schools, and themselves.

We worked hard when it was time to work, and I felt good about the team, even though I figured that Miami was better than anybody we had played, except perhaps Florida. I felt our best chance to win might rest with the kicking game, where I thought we had a distinct edge.

I've been asked many times about our defensive game plan, because of the way our people swarmed all over Vinny Testaverde, the great Miami passer. Well, frankly, necessity *is* the mother of invention. We had, of course, looked at a number of game films, and in staff meetings we had all agreed that if Vinny Testaverde had enough time, he could beat anybody. He is a truly fine passer. I watched him during warm-ups before the game, and he was throwing those nice, tight spirals that you see only the great ones throw. Joe Namath threw them; so did Tony Robinson. Coach Donahue and his staff spent untold hours developing the plan to take the game away from Testaverde. It is a credit to their abilities that they were able to come up with so many stunts and blitzes we had never shown. That put the Miami offense out of synch.

Walt Harris and his offensive staff had a good game plan, too;

and we were able to move the ball well after the first couple of possessions allowed them to fine tune it. Neverthelesss, a football team isn't just defense or offense or kicking; it's all the component parts coming together. Ours all came together in this game. I didn't expect us to beat Miami by such a lopsided score, 35–7, but this Tennessee team was a unique one. To use an overused phrase, it was a team of destiny.

The game itself—Daryl Dickey's scrambling pass to Jeff Smith for a touchdown, the sacks of Testaverde, the interceptions, Jeff Powell's long run—all these plays are on film and videotape for Tennessee fans to enjoy over and over again. Yet there are moments in time that are very special. They come and go and can't be recaptured. I sometimes wonder if there ever again will be another night like that one in the Superdome.

Those thousands and thousands of wonderful Tennessee fans, all that orange wherever you looked, Dr. W. J. Julian's magnificent Pride of the Southland Band playing "Rocky Top"—it all made a difference. We are supposed to stay apart from the hoopla on the sidelines, but I'll admit that I was caught up in it. So were the players and the other coaches.

It was a wonderful ending to a magnificent, championship year.

We had suffered our one loss early in the season and, with two ties as well, we never had been in any contention for the number one spot in the rankings. In fact, we didn't hit the top ten until after the regular season was finished. Consequently we knew there was no realistic hope that we would be a factor in the national championship picture. I have no quarrel with the polls; the teams that finished ahead of us had slightly better overall records. But on January 1, 1986, Tennessee was as good as any university football team in the nation.

During the plane trip back to Knoxville the next day, I thought of how this really wasn't Johnny Majors' team. No team belongs to the head coach. It was Tennessee's team. It belonged to the university, the players, and the fans. This group of players made it a happy homecoming for us all.

Hundreds of people met us at the airport. As we rode back to Knoxville along Alcoa Highway, thousands of people waved and cheered and honked their horns. Once back at the university, there was a campus celebration and lots of television interviews. The stars of the game were treated like the heroes they were. It was the perfect ending to a perfect week.

The ties binding me to Tennessee were stronger than ever.

Football is a lot more than the good times. The hard work, the bad breaks, and the disappointing losses are all a part of the big picture. They help us grow.

But we need the great moments now and then, and the week of the 1986 Sugar Bowl will always be one of my richest memories. For thousands of Tennessee fans also, it will be remembered as one of the best times of their lives.

After all the hoopla was over and it was time to go home, Mary Lynn and I walked out to our car and sighed deeply. "Have you ever seen so many people have such a good time?" she reflected.

"No," I responded. "I've never seen so many happy people before, during, and after any game."

And we went home.

·36·

Aiming for the Best

There never has been a time when the college athlete has not faced temptations. There never will be such a time, either. For the most part, athletes face the same problems other students confront. When an athlete is involved, though, it often becomes page one news. That's just the way it is. We are highly visible. The most frightening danger on the current scene is drugs.

My generation, at least where I was reared, knew nothing about drugs. They were outside the realm of our experience. I wish children today could be brought up in that same innocent atmosphere.

But drugs are here. They are a part of the scene, and we can't wish them away. Teenagers and young adults always have faced strong peer pressure, and I'm sure that college football players feel that pressure like most other students.

In January of 1986 two of our former football players, Tony Robinson and B. B. Cooper, were arrested by Knoxville police and charged with selling cocaine to an undercover officer. As this is written they still are awaiting trial and, obviously, I cannot make any comments here on the outcome of those proceedings.

I was in Hawaii coaching the East All-Star team in the Hula Bowl when the story broke. My first reaction was one of shock. I had no reason to suspect that either one of them might be involved in anything related to drugs and, of course, I have no personal knowledge that they were. I hope they weren't. Since verdicts of guilt or innocence are determined by the process of law, and since I knew nothing about the case, I had no business trying either to defend or convict them.

I will say that when they were on our football squad, they never were disciplinary problems. They followed the training rules like everyone else on the team does. Tony Robinson was our most heralded player until he was injured in mid-season, the most talented quarterback I have ever coached. Tony is a likeable young man, rather quiet, but with a lot of self-confidence. He never gave anyone on my staff any problems, including me.

B. B. Cooper was a favorite of mine when he played for us in 1981–1984. He was a walk on who won a scholarship by hard effort, and I always admire the kids who get it the hard way. A short, chunky guy, he was an outstanding blocker and a decent runner at fullback. He was an excellent student, majoring in engineering. He comes from a strong academic background; both his parents are college teachers.

I was a bit upset that the news media had been tipped off in advance of the arrest. The people we all want put out of business are the ones who control the operation. I wondered if some higher-ups could have been nabbed if there hadn't been leaks to the media because two well-known athletes were allegedly involved.

Their arrest made headlines throughout the South and prompted all of us at the University of Tennessee to take a closer look at our drug prevention program. As far as we have been able to tell, we do not have a drug problem on the football squad or, for that matter, on any of the teams at Tennessee. Our testing program is being stepped up to include more spot checks, and we stay in touch with developments in drug programs at other schools.

I am in favor of a strong drug program in prevention, testing, and rehabilitation. We have experts come in each year to talk with the squad about drug abuse. We have done this since drugs became a widespread problem.

People in college sports have the opportunity to lead the way in this fight, I believe. Professional sports seem to have this problem on a much larger scale than college does, but its hands seem to be somewhat tied by players' unions and contractural tangles.

My own gut reaction is to come down hard on violators. I've told the squad I have no sympathy for anybody found dealing in drugs. However, everybody makes mistakes in life, and being self-righteous about drugs will not help matters. The first step should be to educate and prevent. That saves everybody a lot of trouble. But we are talking about human beings, and if a player makes a mistake he deserves the chance to rehabilitate himself.

It's like everything else in college football: the player should come first.

Another problem in college football, and one we always are going to have with us, is the overzealous booster who goes beyond the rules of the National Collegiate Athletic Association in dealing with student athletes.

Recently the Knoxville and Nashville newspapers conducted investigations of the Tennessee sports program after a credit card belonging to a Vol booster was found in Tony Robinson's car as an offshoot of the drug arrest. Certain allegations of booster involvement with football and basketball players were printed, and Dr. Boling formed a committee to conduct an internal investigation into these charges and any others that may arise. As in the drugs case, there had been no final disposition of the matter at the time this book went to press, and I don't feel I should discuss any of the specific allegations here. However, I can discusss the general subject of rules violations.

Some people say that no school can abide by the NCAA rules because they're too complex. I disagree with them. The rulebook is technical, and it is complicated, and sometimes rules are broken in complete innocence; but still the main thrust of the code is clear. Coaches have the responsibility to know what they can and cannot do, and we also have the responsibility to let our supporters know how we stand on the subject of cheating or not cheating. Tennessee boosters know that we have made an effort to run a clean program and want it kept that way.

Booster activity is one of the most difficult things for a school to control. Every Vol supporter has the potential of getting the University of Tennessee in trouble.

Under NCAA rules it is illegal for an athlete to get anything extra that the average student doesn't get, except for the tuition, books, room, and board that go with the athletic grant-in-aid.

Nevertheless some supporters want to do things for athletes. Some do them with good intentions, because they simply like to help people. Others do them because doing favors for athletes makes them feel important, and still others do them because they want their school to win. Even if the coaches and school officials are totally unaware of these illegal activities, under NCAA bylaws the institution must accept the responsibility. Even though it seems unfair, there simply is no other way to handle the issue.

Regardless of the outcome of Tennessee's internal investigation, I believe we will be an even stronger organization in the future. Nobody enjoys going through this kind of experience, but at least it makes us take a long, close look at everything that could affect our program. We'll continue to try to make the public and our supporters aware of our policy, which is that we intend to live within the rules. Period. No exceptions.

Investigative reporting by newspapers is the "in" thing these days, and as long as it is done objectively I don't see why anyone would have any objection to it. I wonder, though, if some reporters sometimes look so hard for the juicy, bad stuff that they ignore the positive side of their stories. There were times this past winter when it seemed as if that was the case at Tennessee.

Once I realized what was taking place, I decided to take no hand in matters while the newspaper investigations were in process. I knew that reporters were calling some former players and coaches, but I didn't talk with these people or try to tell anybody what to say. I knew I had nothing to hide. Some of them later called me to complain that some of the reporters—not all of them—quoted them only when it seemed to suit their purpose and left out the good things they had said about our program. Some of them also said that certain reporters got abusive when the answers didn't suit them. Thus it seems that the objectivity of the individual reporter has a lot to do with whether a newspaper investigation is conducted objectively.

Academics is another concern of coaches and sports administrators. A movement is currently afoot toward establishing higher academic standards for scholarship athletes, and new NCAA standards go into effect with the next recruiting class. New standards were adopted by the University of Tennessee two years ago, however. I do not quarrel with the drive for higher graduation percentages among college athletics.

I do hope, however, that in the quest for higher academic standards we don't shut the door completely to those kids who have been disadvantaged in their primary and secondary school backgrounds. I have seen many of these young men, many of them minority students, beat the odds. They come in as borderline cases, hang on by their toenails for a while, and then surprise us by making it in the classroom as well as on the football field.

I feel good about Tennessee's academic program. Our graduation rate is moving steadily upward, and we encourage those players who have completed their eligibility to stay on until they graduate. We usually find something for them to do in the athletic program while they are completing their studies. We have had student-athletes graduate from every college of the university except the College of Nursing, and our players are becoming better students every year. In the fall quarter of 1985, there was only one failing grade reported in our entire freshman football class, an enviable statistic for any group of students of the same size.

Thanks to Doug Dickey, I was able to devote full time to recruiting and spring practice while the furor over the drug arrests and the newspaper allegations was at its height. With some athletic directors, I might have been up to my head in meetings and conferences, but Doug took many of those matters on himself and left me free to worry about the football team.

Doug has been a tremendous help to me since he took over as athletic director in September of 1985. I might as well admit that I had some reservations when it was first suggested that he might be the one to replace Bob Woodruff. The reason wasn't that I had anything against Doug, but I just wasn't sure if it would work or not. Doug was a former coach himself—one of the best—and I didn't know if he would be looking over my shoulder when I went to the blackboard. Coaches can be a little touchy at times.

A year or so earlier I had told the university administration that I would be interested in the dual job of head football coach and athletic director when Bob Woodruff retired. I knew that it had worked well with some others, such as Neyland, Bryant, and Dooley, and any coach naturally would like to be his own boss.

When Bear Bryant had two or three off seasons in the late '60s, rumors started going around that he was geting too old. The word was that Alabama was going to let him go. Finally he called a press conference.

"The athletic director and I have discussed this matter," he announced, "and we have decided that I'm going to stay on as coach. Now I don't want to hear any more about it."

Dr. Boling told me that it was his policy not to combine the two jobs, and that was that. I see no point in getting upset over things we cannot control; life is too short as it is. And if I could hold down only one of the two jobs, there never was any doubt about which one I wanted that to be. I hope to go on coaching for many years.

Any misgivings I had about the situation were eased after I talked to people who knew both Doug and me. To a person, they agreed that we could work together well, and that has been the case. Doug has had a number of difficulties thrown at him since he took over as athletic director, but he has faced all of it positively. I believe his ideas for improving facilities and raising funds have alread set the groundwork for a powerful future for Tennessee athletics.

One of Doug's favorite sayings is, "In this business, if you're standing still you're losing ground." On that we are in full agreement, and I believe the Tennessee program is moving forward in very capable hands.

As a former coach, Doug knows the value of putting the team first. I like the way he summed up our 1985 championship season. "It's amazing what can happen when nobody cares who gets the credit," he said.

I agree.

·37·

Just Call Me Coach

Sometimes people say to me, "I wouldn't have your job for anything."

Well, I've got news for them. I wouldn't swap jobs with anybody.

To me, coaching is the most interesting, most challenging, most exciting profession in the world. I'll admit that it has its tough moments, but what worthwhile work doesn't?

I love everything about coaching. I love the thrill of game day, with the big crowds and the colors and the marching bands; the eternal chess game of offense versus defense; the X's and O's; the big plays that erupt suddenly and turn the momentum from one team to the other. I love it all.

I enjoy staff meetings, reviewing films, and all the other details of preparing for a game. I even enjoy recruiting. After almost thirty years of doing it, I still welcome the challenge of hitting the road and trying to convince young men just coming out of high school that the University of Tennessee is the best place for them. I must have something of the ham in me because I even enjoy public appearances, television shows, and press interviews.

Most of all, I love the pure coaching part of the job, teaching on the practice field. Coaching is nothing more and nothing less than teaching, and I have always regarded myself first and foremost as a teacher. To play a part in the development of a young man, both as an athlete and as a person, is one of the most gratifying experiences that anyone can have.

As a head coach, I miss the close contact I used to have with the players on the practice field. Ironically, the more successful a program becomes, the less opportunity the head coach has to engage in hands-on teaching. A successful program means a good staff, and if he has a good staff the smart head coach leaves the individual and position coaching up to the assistants. I realize this, and I try to stay out of the way as much as possible. Every now and then, though, I'll jump in there just to keep from going to seed.

Basically, I am an optimist. I don't, however, believe in the Pollyanna approach. I never have taken a head coaching job with any promise, spoken or implied, to win a certain number of games in a certain number of years, not at Iowa State, not at Pittsburgh, and not at Tennessee. What I have always promised is that our teams will play with pride and enthusiasm.

Most coaches have some sort of motto or pet saying that expresses their basic approach to the game. Mine is *Pride and Enthusiasm*. I always add to that, *The Fourth Quarter*. I want our players to feel that the fourth quarter belongs to us. I want them to believe they have worked hard enough, are conditioned well enough, and are prepared soundly enough that they will come through when everything is on the line.

Obviously, we don't win all the close ones. The coaches and players on the other side of the field are striving for the same goals. But the thing that makes me the most proud as a coach is not Iowa State's first bowl appearance, or the 1976 national champioship at Pittsburgh, or the great 1985 season at Tennessee. Instead, what makes me the proudest is the fact that none of our teams has ever rolled over and died. Some of our teams haven't been as good as others, but not one has ever quit.

The first thing that any coaching staff must do is to weed out selfishness. The team always has to be number one, the individual number two. No program can be successful with players who put themselves ahead of the team.

The time when a coach teaches this philosophy is when he first takes a new position. This usually is a very painful time, for players and coaches alike. The players must adjust to different ways and different techniques and, usually, to stricter discipline. The coaches have to get their philosophy across to a large group of young men in a relatively short length of time. I have found, however, that the thoroughly dedicated football player always is able to make the adjustment.

No head coach can be any better than his staff. Nothing is more important to a football program than the assistant coaches. Show me a winning team, and I'll show you a good group of assistant coaches. I have been very fortunate in my head coaching career to have had some great staffs: the young group that broke in together at Iowa State, the ones that played such a big part in the great years at Pittsburgh, and finally my current staff at Tennessee, which I think is as good as any in the nation.

I don't claim to be the easiest head coach in the world to work for. I can get pretty ornery at times. Bad practices upset me. I firmly believe that practice doesn't make perfect; perfect practice does. I know that perfection is something we strive for and never reach, and I'm sure I've demanded too much at times. I've jumped on people and then felt badly about it later. I'm not as bad about that as I used to be. I hope that's because I've mellowed some, not just because we've had better teams the last few years.

I have always tried to impress upon my assistants that my door opens from both directions. If they have something on their minds they think I should know, I want to hear it. While I want loyal coaches, I don't want any yes men. If an assistant thinks I'm wrong about something, I want him to speak his piece. I'll make the final decision and take the responsibility for it, but I want the input from my assistants.

Unselfishness, putting the team first and the individual second, applies to coaches and players alike. Through the years, fortunately, I haven't had to let many coaches go. Nothing is more painful, but if a coach gets in the way of the welfare of the team and the program, the problem has to be faced directly.

I don't want to give the impression that coaching is all grim and steely-eyed. The dedication has to be there, of course, but mostly coaching is fun. Whenever people unite around a common cause, closeness is the first result, and a close group always does a lot of teasing and joking. Usually it is the assistants who create the light moments.

I will always look back on my days at Iowa State with a special fondness. It was my first head coaching position, and I was only in my early thirties. Thus I was more of a contemporary with my assistants than I am now.

On one occasion a high school coach lent us a film to use for studying a prospect. I had made a big point of cautioning the assistants always to make sure that we returned the films we borrowed. We wanted to make a good impression on high school coaches.

I took the film one night and forgot all about it. When we couldn't find it later, I ordered all the coaches' offices turned upside down in a search for it. It was not to be found.

A month or so later, Gordon Smith borrowed my car, opened the trunk to put something in it, and found the film. After all my fussing, I was the culprit!

Then Gordon and I decided to play a trick on Joe Madden. I slipped the film in a lower drawer of Joe's desk while he was out of the office. Later I had him look there under some pretext. "What's that, Joe?" I asked when he opened the door. He handed me the film with a dumbfounded look on his face. He probably had looked through that drawer a dozen times and knew it wasn't supposed to be there. We later told him the truth, but we let him sweat it out first.

Joe Avezzano was one of the most dynamic assistants I ever had. He was a fine field coach and a great recruiter, a bundle of charm and energy. But when Joe first joined our staff at Iowa State, he worried me to death. He was a handsome Italian from Miami, a real cool cat, and he dressed like one. He might show up in a felt hat, dark glasses, mod slacks, and a cape slung over his shoulders. One of our coaches, King Block, had been a cow-puncher, and shortly after I came there we hired Ray Green, my first black coach. Whenever they went to the same social functions, with Joe in his dude suit, King looking like he had just gotten down off Trigger, and Ray in his Afro-American outfit, it looked like a costume party at the United Nations.

Naturally, being in my first head coaching job, I was concerned about the image we were projecting in the heart of middle America. I talked to Joe about it.

"But Coach, this is me. This is Joe Avezzano," he said.

"Yes," I answered, "and this is farmland. Small town, conservative Iowa. We're asking these people to support our program, and we don't want to make it any harder for them to accept us than we have to."

One day my good friend, Arch Steele, our academic counselor, called me. "We've got a problem," he said. "The school paper is about to print a picture of Joe Avezzano, and after you take a look I'm sure you won't want it published."

I got a copy of the ad for an Ames clothing store, Country Cobbler, and almost fell out of my chair. It showed Joe, nude from the waist up, facing the camera and hugging a topless young lady whose back was to the camera. Joe had his arms around the girl and was holding a football in one hand. The caption read, "Clothes by Country Cobbler, Ball by Avezzano."

Practice was about to start. I covered the three blocks to the field on a dead run, and as soon as I got there I yelled "AVEZ-ZANO!" at the top of my voice. Joe says he'll never forget the look on my face.

"What's wrong?" he asked.

I told him.

"It's too late now," he answered. "The paper's going to press this afternoon."

"Wrong," I responded. "Joe, I'll take the offensive line for you. You get down to that store and find a way to get that picture out of there, or you're fired!"

Joe took off running, and somehow he talked the people at the store into pulling the ad.

As I say, coaching may be demanding, but it is never dull!

Football has changed in many ways since I became a coach, but the underlying basics have remained the same. I still use those old game maxims I learned at Tennessee as a player, starting with "The team that makes the fewest mistakes usually wins."

The things that were true in General Neyland's time are just as true today. If I were asked to give advice to the coaches just coming into the profession, it would be to get back to the basics. It seems to me that too many of the younger coaches nowadays are long on chalk talk and short on fundamentals. They can do wonders with the X's and O's on the blackboard, and I'm not knocking that. However, the most important coaching is still done on the practice field. The winning edge that everybody talks about so much usually turns out to be old fashioned blocking and tackling.

The head coaches I have always admired the most are men like my father, Bowden Wyatt, Bear Bryant, and Vince Lombardi. They were tough, demanding, hard-nosed fundamentalists. Players may hate them at times on the practice field, but they love them the rest of their lives.

When I was a young assistant coach, I often studied National Football League films to increase my knowledge of the game. While the pros played a very exciting brand of football then, the truth is that they didn't have a lot of good, old-fashioned blocking and tackling until Lombardi came along at Green Bay in the mid-60's. There always will be a place in football for the man who stresses the basics and—pardon my Tennessee heritage again—emphasizes the kicking game.

Football may be a trivial pursuit to some people; we all have different sets of values. To me football is the land of opportunity. Too few things in this country are as democratic as football. Wealth and social status mean nothing on the football field; effort and unselfishness mean everything. The game has opened many doors, which otherwise might have stayed shut, to thousands of young men, both black and white. And for the coach, football gives the opportunity to touch and be touched by many people in all walks of life.

I hope to be involved in college athletics, one way or another, for as long as I live. I certainly intend to go on coaching as long as I have the health and zest for it. I am also fully aware that today's hero can be tomorrow's goat. As my old friend, Barry Switzer, says, "In this business, you're never more than seven days away from humility."

Or, as Clay Stapleton used to say, "Your personality will take you to September."

My father retired at sixty-five because he was forced to do so, but he never really adjusted to it. His home was on the football field.

So is mine. Right here at the University of Tennessee.